RENTING YOUR RECREATIONAL PROPERTY FOR PROFIT

Heather Bayer

Self-Counsel Press
(a division of)
International Self-Counsel Press Ltd.
USA   Canada

Self-Counsel Press acknowledges the financial support of the Government of Canada through the Book Publishing Industry Development Program (BPIDP) for our publishing activities.

Printed in Canada.

Second edition: 2007

Library and Archives Canada Cataloguing in Publication

    Bayer, Heather, 1955–
Renting your recreational property for profit / Heather Bayer.—
2nd ed.

Includes a CD-ROM.
1st edition had title: Renting for profit.
ISBN 978-1-55180-733-1

    1. Vacation rentals — Handbooks, manuals, etc. I. Bayer,
Heather, 1955– Renting for profit. II. Title.
HD1394.B394 2007   333.33'8   C2006-906687-6

ANCIENT FOREST
FRIENDLY

Self-Counsel Press
(a division of)
International Self-Counsel Press Ltd.

1704 North State Street   1481 Charlotte Road
Bellingham, WA 98225   North Vancouver, BC V7J 1H1
USA   Canada

CONTENTS

6 EMERGENCIES AND CONTINGENCIES

7 BOOKING SYSTEMS

8 SEASONAL RENTALS

SAMPLES

TABLE

INTRODUCTION

WHY SHOULD YOU READ THIS BOOK?

Whether you are planning to rent your vacation home for the first time, buying a property as an investment, or already have second home rental income and want to know how to increase it, this is the book for you. The principal aim of *Renting Your Recreational Property for Profit* is to provide you with a wealth of information to help you be successful in renting your property. The information and anecdotes in the book have come from my own experiences renting cottages in both England and Canada over the last fifteen or so years, as well as invaluable contributions from owners and renters alike, who between them have racked up years of rental know-how.

If you've had your recreational home for a number of years and are now thinking of renting for the first time to provide additional income, you may have to look at it from a different viewpoint and be prepared to make some tough decisions. What you may have considered acceptable quirks of the cabin, cottage, villa, or condo will have to be dealt with or fixed, the worn furniture replaced, and kitchen appliances updated. This book will help you with those decisions, provide checklists to make sure you don't overlook anything, and offer advice on preparing for successful rental.

There will be plenty of choices to make in terms of where you will advertise and how to manage a marketing budget; whether it is in your best interest to use a rental agency or manage the renting yourself; and who will look after the property when you are not there. This book draws on experiences of owners with all types of rentals, from those who manage every part of their business, to owners living halfway round the world who rely on rental and property management agencies to look after their properties.

To help you with the operational side of your rental business, the CD that accompanies this book contains a rental planning kit with templates you can customize to suit your own needs. The forms include rental agreements, booking forms, client surveys, and a wealth of additional information.

Armed with your copy of *Renting Your Recreational Property for Profit,* you will be able to maximize the rental potential of your vacation property and have great fun running your own rental business.

1
IS RENTING FOR YOU?

Second home ownership is booming across North America and year on year, real estate companies are reporting rising interest in the purchase of vacation homes with rental potential.

In the US, the National Association of Realtors (NAR), in a review of the 2003 census, found 43.8 million second homes, of which 6.6 million were determined to be vacation homes. NAR says 23 percent of all homes purchased in 2004 were for investment purposes, and another 13 percent were vacation homes. Sales of investment homes were up about 14 percent from 1.57 million in 2003, with sales of vacation homes rising to 1.02 million, up almost 20 percent from the 850,000 sold in 2003.

The Canadian vacation home market continues to boom, with 40 percent of prospective purchasers planning on renting out their property to help cover some of the costs. Realtor Royal LePage reports, "Low interest rates, people redirecting their investment dollars from the stock market into recreational real estate, and

Americans buying slices of Canadian recreational paradise are the compelling factors that are sustaining demand."

The typical recreational or second home owner is a baby boomer, so there is a good likelihood that sales of these properties will remain high over the next decade as this generation approaches retirement age. There are also indications that more people in their thirties and forties are investing in recreational home real estate, not only to provide for their economic future but to support the growing trend to stay fairly close to home for vacation time and to bring family together in a safe and known environment.

THE COSTS OF RECREATIONAL HOME OWNERSHIP

The rush to find the perfect waterfront property has forced many people to buy earlier than they anticipated just to be assured of their future retirement dream. For those who have chosen this path, recreational property ownership comes at a price, as the initial investment and furnishing costs are closely and relentlessly followed by a welter of expenses. Some of these are expected and budgeted for; others come as a surprise. A sheared water line; the need for water softener or purification systems; winterizing; maintaining decking and sidings; prevention of water ingress in spring — these are just some of the challenges faced by owners I spoke to during the research for this book. In most cases, even where owners had substantial contingency funds, the additional expenses of recreational property ownership — including spiraling electrical costs and property taxes — came as quite a shock.

So, as reality overshadows the initial enthusiasm for the purchase, many new owners and significant numbers of seasoned owners will consider renting their recreational property to offset these costs. Meanwhile, others have deliberately bought property to take advantage of the investment opportunity and the potential for rental income, which is clearly there for high-season weeks.

What can you realistically achieve from renting your property? The simple answer is that you will not make your fortune — unless, of course, you buy several properties, renovate them, rent them for a time, and resell them — but that's the subject of another book!

Renting Your Recreational Property for Profit will explain how, by giving careful consideration to marketing, property management, guest services, and added value, you can make enough money to pay the bills, meet the mortgage payments, do the routine maintenance and repairs, and have a surplus to make improvements that will ultimately increase the value of your property and the pleasure you get out of owning it. In short, this book is about maximizing the investment you've made so the return amply covers the expenses. Renting your recreational property requires work. It's not enough to scour yard sales for bargain furniture, place a small ad in a couple of newspapers, then sit back and wait for the money to roll in. Making a profit from vacation rental requires sound planning and forward thinking, and of course adopting some of the tips from this book.

IS RENTING FOR YOU OR NOT?

You have probably invested a lot in your recreational property. That investment is in money and time, and for many people it is also an emotional investment. Maybe you've owned a cottage for many years, or it has been in the family for a long time. That property holds many happy and precious memories of fun, laughter, sunshine, and relaxation. Or perhaps you are a new owner, enjoying the wonderful feeling of owning your own piece of paradise that you can return to after a long week in the city. Perhaps you've bought the property for your retirement and visit occasionally to dream and imagine what it will be like when you can be up at the cottage full time.

Opening your place in the country to strangers often raises emotional issues. You imagine them inhabiting your precious space, using your bedrooms, watching your TV, and sitting on your deck enjoying your sunsets. For some people, the very thought makes renting a nonstarter. If the weeks your vacation home is rented fill you with dread — if you worry that damage is being done, your watercraft are being wrecked, and candle wax will be spilled on your oak table, then renting is probably not for you.

In an ideal world, of course, you would rent your property only to lovely families who leave it in immaculate condition, come back year after year, and tell their friends, who also look after your place as you would. If you really work at it, you can get as close as possible to this ideal. Even so, it's probably better to accept that there will always be the odd group who, on first vetting, seemed just the right renters, but let you down all the same. This happens very occasionally, and I'm not going to pretend it doesn't. But by using the checklists you'll find in this book and on the CD-ROM, asking the right questions, and planning carefully, you will definitely lessen the risk of attracting the renters from hell!

Renting your cottage should, and can be, a pleasurable and profitable experience, allowing you to make the most of your investment by having it earn money for you when you are not using it. To ensure that your rental venture is a success, you'll need to do some essential groundwork, careful research, and thorough planning. With the right systems in place, you can have peace of mind knowing that your guests are respecting your piece of paradise as if it were their own. They will want to come back year after year, so will make sure it is well looked after.

With good marketing, you should be able to rent your cottage throughout the high-season weeks prevalent in your area. For many this will be July and August, Spring break, all the long weekends, and possibly Christmas and New Year's. This makes for at least 12 weeks of high-season income if you don't use the property yourself during any of those times. If your property is in an area with a longer high-season — perhaps with both great fall color and a long ski season, you will achieve a higher rate of occupancy. With ever-increasing demand for vacation properties to rent, this level of occupancy should pose no difficulty. The challenge lies in filling the low-season weeks and weekends and getting your property to work for you all year round. This book is designed help you to do that.

But before we get into the details that will lead you to a profitable rental business, just take a few minutes to reflect on the following sad tale. Admittedly this is a worst-case scenario: You would never expect all the situations described here to happen in the course of just one rental. However, every incident described here has actually been experienced by one or more of the vacation rental owners who contributed to this book. Consider this a cautionary tale about what can happen if you don't pay sufficient attention to the details and rely on luck rather than sound judgment in planning your rentals.

This is the story of a new recreational property owner who decided that renting his property for a few weekends and weeks in the summer would provide him with enough income to pay some bills, and maybe have some money left over for improvements. Let's for a moment imagine that person is you …

Nightmare rental weekend

It's the first long weekend of the summer and you arrive at your vacation home to see your first guests in, excited at the prospect and eager to meet them and show off your special place. You had received many responses to your ad in *The Star*, but had decided to rent to the first person who phoned because she sounded so nice — a real family person. She said they'd arrive by 4 p.m. on Friday, so you've taken an afternoon off work to get there in plenty of time to check that everything's in place for their arrival. Six o'clock passes, seven, then eight, and still they don't show up. There are no messages on your voice mail, and no answer at their home phone. Now you are worried. Have they had an accident? Are they lost? Should you stay, although you need to get back home to the family? At least you got a deposit from them. But you had said it would be OK for them to pay the balance on arrival — perhaps not such a good idea now. And … darn … you told them you'd wait, so didn't let them know where the key would be. So you'll just have to sit it out.

Just a few more … and the dog!

Just as you are beginning to despair, the phone rings. The guests stopped off to see friends on the way and are now totally lost, as they forgot to bring the directions you gave them over the phone last week. They are over an hour away and are not going to arrive much before 11 p.m. Irritated and annoyed, you settle back to wait. A van finally pulls into the driveway at 11:30 p.m., spilling out three more people than you were expecting. On the phone, your contact had said it would be her and her husband and their three children, but on your doorstep, and piling into the house, are five children and a third adult. Airily they tell you that the renter's sister decided to join them at the last minute. They didn't think you would mind, and the kids are all happy to bunk in together. You do mind, particularly when you see a small dog being unloaded from the van along with the luggage. They hadn't mentioned a dog. But neither had you!

It's late, though, you've got a long drive home, and you need to explain some of the quirkier bits of cottage living they may not have encountered before. Eager to get the children settled, the moms go off, and you go through the list you've prepared with dad. He assures you he'll go through it in the morning and call you if he has any questions. Feeling a little uneasy about the whole business, you set off back to the city wondering if renting really was such a good idea after all.

Emergency calls

You are woken by the phone at 6 a.m. — you've only been home since three! The cottage toilet is blocked and overflowing and they can't find a plunger. What next? You need to call out a local plumber but it's a holiday weekend, so you spend the rest of the morning on the phone looking for someone willing to take an emergency call-out without charging the earth. Having tracked down a plumber, you call the cottage to let the guests know he's on his way, only to be told that most of the family has gone to the local emergency room as one of the children slipped on the broken deck step and may have broken an ankle. You had meant to mention the step last night — it will be fixed on Monday — but in the confusion over their late arrival you forgot to warn them. Your guests are very unhappy and suggest they might pursue an insurance claim against you for not making it clear the step was dangerous. Now, your anxiety levels are really rising!

Plumbing sucks!

At midday, the plumber calls; there had clearly been much more than human waste going down the toilet, despite you having explained what the consequences would be. Just for good measure, the plumber adds that the septic tank needs emptying — it looks dangerously full and there is the beginning of that telltale odor around the septic bed. You've only had the property a couple of months, and the previous owners had told you they emptied it every five years and it was done about three years ago. Not being used to the finer points of septic and plumbing systems, you hadn't given it much thought, but now you need to. When you tell the plumber to go ahead and make arrangements to empty the septic tank, he advises that in the interim the toilet should be flushed only when really required or the problem will get worse. Now you'll need to speak to your guests again.

How not to get to know the neighbors

Just as you are about to call your guests, the phone rings again. It's your neighbors on the lake. You've met them once or twice — a pleasant couple who run a small resort of five cottages. They have a lovely beach area for their clients with a range of watercraft — canoes, pedal boats, kayaks, and rowboats, and are very proud of the new water slide they have put in alongside their swimming raft. Unfortunately, they explain that your guests' children have taken over the waterslide and raft, preventing their own guests from using it. When they spoke to the parents, apparently they were met with complete indifference: "They are kids and just having fun; we can't keep at them all day long." Your neighbors, although quite calm, are clearly upset and ask you to talk with your renters and firmly tell them that the waterslide and raft are the property of the resort and should not be used by their children. Just as you are about to end the call, your neighbor adds that one of the adults in your party has just taken out one of the resort canoes; please can you act quickly!

Willing yourself to keep your cool, you phone the cottage. The line is busy, as it is when you call again — and again. An hour later, you've still failed to get through, so you phone the neighbors again to explain. This time their annoyance is really apparent — the children are still occupying the swimming raft and using the boats. You really need to do something. This is not how it was supposed to be. And as you worry about what to do next, you remember that in your haste to get away last night, you forgot to ask for the rest of the rental money and the damage deposit. What a mess!

Fortunately, the next time you phone you reach someone, but when you explain about your neighbors' concerns, you find it's too late — your renter is complaining because the neighbor has shouted at his children and told them to stay off the raft. Your renter says your advertisement mentioned a swimming raft, and they had assumed it was a shared one. It's clear this is getting out of hand, so you apologize for your neighbor's anger and point out the swimming raft for your place has the cottage name clearly painted on the side.

Finally able to calm everyone down, you go back to your neighbor and assure him you've made it clear to your guests what is available to them and what is not. He suggests that maybe you hire a caretaker to look after your cottage, someone who could be on hand to deal with problems when they arise. You begin to realize this is just one of the things you'll have to think seriously about if you are ever to rent your property again.

Of course, this is a worst-case scenario. It is very unlikely that you would have to face nearly that many problems during just one guest weekend. However, each one of these problems could have been prevented with forethought and good planning. This book will deal with all of these and more, so your rental experience can run smoothly and successfully. You will still encounter difficult clients and experience the occasional challenging situation, but if you follow the advice and tips contained in this book, you will be far better able to deal with any situation that may arise, and you'll have contingency plans in place to cover almost any eventuality.

2
THE BIG QUESTIONS

If you've made the decision that you are going to take the vacation home rental business seriously, you'll need to know where to start. It's time to ask yourself some searching questions, and this is probably best done with the whole family involved. Some decisions may affect how much time you will spend on the rental enterprise, as well as how much income you will generate, and others will affect your family (as would any other business you run from your home). If you are intending to handle the renting alone, family members should be part of the decision-making process from the outset. Take some time thinking this through. Once you've started the ball rolling, it's difficult to stop!

This chapter addresses some key questions to ask yourself. The CD includes a form, To Rent or Not to Rent, for you to respond to these questions and add more of your own.

WHAT DO I WANT TO GET OUT OF IT?

Not just money, but personal satisfaction, enjoyment of helping people with planning their vacation, and the challenge of marketing and achieving rental objectives are a few of the goals you might wish to aim for. If you have not been involved in a small business before, you might not have considered the importance of knowing where you want to get before you plan the steps to get there. The section on setting goals gives more ideas on how to tackle this question.

HOW MUCH TIME DO I WANT TO SPEND DOING THIS?

An hour a week, two hours, a day, or more? The decisions you make about renting your recreational home will determine, to some extent, how much time you will need to devote to make it a success. If you have created or are planning to create your own website, it will need continual updating to make sure it is rated highly on search engines; managing your own bookings means being in constant touch with your clients, confirming reservations, handling money, and keeping the paperwork up to date; and during the rental season, considerable time will be needed to look after the property between rentals.

DO I WANT TO MARKET THE RENTALS MYSELF OR USE A RENTAL AGENCY?

The answer to this question may follow naturally from the answer to the question above. If you don't have sufficient time or inclination to deal with promoting your rental property and dealing with potential and confirmed guests, then you might want to hand over that task to an agency. There is a hefty cost implication here — one you need to consider carefully — as an agency can take up to 40 percent of the income. The section on choosing the right rental agency has suggestions on researching the agency that will work with you best, and includes a list of questions you should ask. If you want to do the marketing yourself — which can be very satisfying — go to the sections on marketing strategy; creating your own website; developing your own brochure and stationery; advertising; and choosing Internet advertising options.

WHO WILL LOOK AFTER THE PROPERTY WHEN I'M NOT THERE?

When you choose to manage renting your vacation home yourself, deciding who will look after it when you are away is a really important question. At the outset, many owners are happy to drive up to the place for a few hours on a Saturday to do a "clean and turnaround" before the next renters arrive. This will save on expenses, but is it really worth it in the long run? And who will handle emergencies? Chapter 10 helps with this dilemma and gives some sound advice on choosing the right person to take on the responsibility of property management.

HOW WILL I TAKE BOOKINGS?

It's easy to think, "Hey, I'm only renting a few weeks a year, why do I need a booking system?" If you are extremely well organized, you may be right, but the pitfalls of accommodation provision — double booking, no-shows, late cancellation, etc. — can adversely affect even the smallest setup. The simple booking system suggested in Chapter 7 and the adaptable templates included on the CD will help you to keep the paperwork organized and reduce the potential for mistakes.

CAN THE COTTAGE BE RENTED YEAR-ROUND AND IF SO, WHAT ARE THE IMPLICATIONS?

If your cottage has a potential for year-round rental it is probably a good idea to exploit this. However, in many locations winter rentals bring a whole range of issues that are not a consideration in the summer. Marketing out-of-season rentals also brings with it additional challenges as the market becomes overloaded with available cottages, and there are fewer people wanting to rent. Chapter 8, Seasonal Rentals, and Chapter 9, Marketing Your Vacation Home, offer ideas that will raise your cottage profile above the competition and attract those hard-to-find guests.

HOW MUCH AM I WILLING TO SPEND TO INCREASE THE RENTAL OPPORTUNITIES?

Although location and the condition of the waterfront go a long way to determining the rental rate, the inside of your rental property can also have a major effect on the price you can reasonably charge. Setting a rate is not just a matter of looking at what the market will stand. It also requires an objective look at what you are really offering and whether it would be economically sound to make any improvements. Chapter 5, Getting Ready for Renting, provides useful advice on adding value, not just for renting during the high-demand times of year, but also for attracting guests throughout the off-season.

WHAT ARE THE TAX AND INSURANCE IMPLICATIONS OF RENTING?

This is a question to ask your accountant and your insurance broker, and one to consider early on in the planning process. There are implications not only in terms of personal taxation, but also in the status of the property should you come to sell it in the future. Insurance companies view vacation rentals differently than single-occupancy residences, and you may find that your current provider will not cover a second home for vacation rental. Some insurers will have stipulations that you may find unworkable, so it is important for you to tackle this issue well before you get set up for renting. There is a brief summary of the issues you need to be aware of and links to more information on the accompanying CD.

HOW WILL THIS AFFECT MY FAMILY?

Do your grown-up children see the cottage in the same way as you do — as an investment rather than a place to go to with friends at a moment's notice? If not, this may be a major issue to sort out. Will your family help in "the business" or be an obstacle to it? Are they prepared to answer the phone as it constantly rings in the winter when potential renters vie to book prime dates? Is everyone prepared for strangers using their beds, sound systems, etc.?

Family "buy-in" may well be a deal breaker, so bring family members in on the discussion early on, or you'll find the problems arising when you least want them to — right in the middle of a rental season.

3
SETTING GOALS

"The sooner you start getting some of what you really want, the more energy you'll have to go for the rest of it."

— Barbara Sher,
Wishcraft — How to Get What You Really Want

If you are going to treat renting your recreational home as a business, think like a business owner would. No company expecting to make a profit would dream of moving into a new venture without a lot of planning. This planning consists of focusing on the current situation, having a clear vision of how things should look in the future, and then making decisions on what has to be done to move toward that goal.

Meaningful goals should meet two basic rules:

1. *A goal is concrete.* It will have a factual outcome, an amount, and a time, and it is grounded in reality. It is not an emotional issue.

2. *A goal is what you really want.* Take some time to imagine what it will be like when you have achieved your goal. Check whether you are comfortable with that, or whether your decision raises any more questions. This emotional side of your goal-setting exercise is an essential part of it, even if you have bought your cottage as an investment and don't see renting as having particular emotional significance.

YOUR VISION

Start by thinking about what is currently happening with your recreational property. Maybe it's been in the family for years and you have just decided to rent, or you've just bought it and have a lot of expenses to manage. You might have been renting it for some time but feel that you could make more income from it. Whatever your situation, just take a moment and make some notes on where you are now, where you want to be, and how you plan on getting there. Sample 1 shows how this simple exercise works.

First, set your goals, then write them down! This is the first part of what will become your rental plan — a miniature business plan — and subsequently your marketing plan. Don't lose sight of the fact that you have decided to do this seriously and, with that in mind, you need to begin with a firm foundation. Use the Creating a Vision Worksheet on the CD to write down your goals for renting your recreational property.

When you've set your goals, remember to keep them at the forefront of your mind. Doubts may set in occasionally — you will perhaps ask yourself whether you are really doing the right thing, and you'll need to revisit your original motives to reaffirm your commitment to renting. Skipping this part of the planning process would be a bit like setting sail in a boat without a rudder — directionless.

SAMPLE 1
CREATING A VISION

Where are we now?	Where do we want to be?	How do we get there?
• Rental at $1,250 per week • Renting six weeks per year • Letting family and friends use cottage for free in high season • Cottage has old mismatched furniture • Expenses (including mortgage) of $1,200 per month	• Rental at $1,500 per week • Renting minimum 14 weeks per year • Family and friends still happy • Meeting 50 percent of monthly costs	• Improve furnishings • Motivate family • Plan better marketing • Create new website • Have family plan/ timeshare option

FINANCIAL GOALS

The majority of vacation home owners rent their properties to gain additional income, so setting clear financial goals from the outset makes a lot of sense.

Take some time to consider how much you want to make annually from renting your property. Don't constrain yourself at the moment by trying to work out if this is feasible. This exercise is more to establish some parameters for you to work with. For example, if you want to make enough money to cover your mortgage payment, that is straightforward to calculate. If you want to fund other expenses, such as winter-proofing the property, adding an additional sleeping cabin, or making major improvements, estimate the costs and then add them all up to give a total. This provides a useful starting point for what follows.

Pete and Anna have a three-bedroom lakefront cottage on Catchacoma Lake in the Kawartha region of Southern Ontario. They bought it partly as an investment, but also to spend the occasional out-of-season weekend there. They plan to rent the cottage for four to five years to raise enough money to build an extension with an additional bedroom and bathroom, rebuild the deck, and replace the roof. They see rental income as the way to achieve their aim of retiring to their cottage while also being able to enjoy time in it before they retire. Taking their plan very seriously, they wrote their financial goals within their strategic plan, setting out short-, intermediate-, and long-term objectives. With these figures they were able to develop a marketing plan that would achieve their goals.

FORECASTING EXPENSES

Financial forecasting consists of identifying your fixed expenses — expenditures you have regardless of whether the property is occupied. These are expenses such as property taxes, telephone rental, insurance, mortgage payments, satellite TV subscription, etc. Some of these costs you will already know — taxes, mortgage payments; others you'll need to think about and make some educated guesses. If you already employ someone to do general maintenance and yard work, include that cost in your fixed expense figure.

Variable costs are those that change dependent on whether the vacation home is occupied or not. For example, cleaning expenses, heating, electricity, and long-distance telephone expenses are variable. By using a spreadsheet program, you can adjust the anticipated expenditures to match your forecast occupancy. The Cottage Rental Calculator (Excel spreadsheet) on the CD shows how this works and allows you to input your own figures.

Capital expenditures

Capital expenditures are one-off costs that may arise during the year. If you have just bought a vacation home there will be expenses to furnish and prepare it (see Chapter 5, Getting Ready for Renting). If your cottage is established, you may need to upgrade it to fit a higher rental category. Chapter 5 also gives some ideas on how to add value to your property for this purpose. Ask yourself what you need to set aside for major purchases through the year, and input this figure on the spreadsheet in the month you expect to make the payment. Don't forget "surprise" expenditures: a septic pump that fails mid-season or a heated water line that needs replacing while you have winter guests in residence, to mention a couple. These might not be planned, so an emergency fund is helpful for such circumstances.

Electrical costs

Let's assume that you are planning to rent year-round. This will mean you'll be heating the property right through the winter, albeit on a minimum setting when it is empty. Be realistic when forecasting electricity costs. Depending on your location, take into account the strain that running air conditioning can place on a budget. The example used in the Rental Calculator on the CD is taken from a four-bedroom cottage heated partly by baseboard heater, partly by a forced-air system, and supplemented by a wood-burning stove. In the example, the electricity costs are spread throughout the year, with an additional amount for winter firewood added in October.

When you are making any forecast, make sure you include all the expenses, as forgetting some could have quite an impact on your break-even calculation. If in doubt, it's better to overestimate expenses now, rather than getting a nasty surprise later.

Don't expect your guests to economize on fuel in the winter or air conditioning in summer, although you can do some things to encourage them to be more thrifty with your power supply. Fitting individual thermostats in each room may help, but you then have to hope they will turn them down when they go out. Saving electricity is often a hit-and-miss affair with guests. Unless you are charging them separately for the fuel they use, why should they bother? Some owners stick a small label onto each thermostat as a reminder; others have a notice on the outer door so that it will be seen as guests leave to go out for the day. This is fine, but from experience, it's sensible to forecast for the worst case: high electricity bills while you have renters in the winter and/or air conditioning units in hot seasons.

"We live about half an hour from our property and drive by regularly. In winter, you can see the back of the place from the road, even more so when the Christmas lights are on. We'd rented it to a group for New Year's, and my husband was incensed each time we went past in the daytime to see all the outside lights on. It was obvious the group hadn't switched the lights off throughout their stay. We've now installed a timer that turns all but one of the exterior lights out at midnight. Not only does this lower the electricity costs, but it's much nicer for our neighbors not to have their night sky polluted by several hundred watts of lighting."

If you have a wood-burning stove or open fireplace, you may need to decide early on in the planning process whether you will provide unlimited wood for your guests to use in the winter, or if you plan to leave a reasonable amount free of charge and expect them to buy additional firewood as required. The first option is more likely to please your guests, and you can increase the winter rental costs accordingly. There's more about adding value to your rental package in Chapter 12, Generating Return Visits.

Telephone

Many owners put a block on long-distance calls and ask guests to use a credit or other calling card. However, others have found that opting for a long distance/international plan with the telephone company gives substantial discounts, while you charge your guests full price for such calls. This works particularly well with overseas guests who do tend to call home quite regularly. When the discount on international calls is anything up to 60 percent, it is well worthwhile allowing unrestricted phone access. Providing it is made very clear on the rental agreement that payment for phone calls will be invoiced after the telephone bill arrives, or deducted from the security deposit, there should be no problem. It's important, however, to hold onto the security deposit until the bill has been received and payment made.

For forecasting purposes, however, simply record the monthly telephone service charges (including any for long distance plans), making the assumption that any call charges will be recouped soon after the bill has been paid.

Satellite TV

Offering full satellite service is definitely a value-added option for winter rentals. You may see your cottage as a getaway from the conveniences of modern life and can't understand why others would want to use their leisure time doing what they do at home; however, there are plenty of people out there who want to do just that.

A cottage owner told me of her amusement when she noticed a party of guests arriving at her property for their summer vacation with a U-Haul trailer containing many of their comforts of home, including a 42-inch TV, DVD player, and assorted game consoles for the children. The two televisions included with the cottage were simply not enough to keep the family occupied!

You may find that your satellite TV provider offers a limited number of free connections/disconnections or changes of viewing packages during a year. If this is the case, you might want to switch off full facilities in the summer and reconnect them in the off-season. Whatever you decide, forecast the expenditure accurately. A note of caution here: make sure any pay-per-view function is either disabled, temporarily disconnected, or password protected or you could find yourself with some very unexpected additional costs!

Property management and maintenance costs

Property management and maintenance costs will depend on whether you will be doing your own management and maintenance, using a dedicated property management company, or a bit of both. Chapter 11, Managing Your Property Yourself, addresses this topic in more detail and will help you understand the benefits and drawbacks of each approach.

For the purposes of this book, the term *rental management* refers to the method you use to look after the rental aspects of the business: advertising; taking bookings; handling deposits, security deposits, and final payments; and looking after the needs of renters while using your property. *Property management* refers to the short- and long-term maintenance requirements: year-round yard work, storm checking, handling emergency problems, etc.

Once you have decided which method will suit you, you'll be in a better position to assess the costs involved. It's usually best to apply a proportion of fixed costs for yard maintenance, which will include mowing and general yard care in the summer and snow clearance in the winter. Naturally, there will be some variation, as the weather plays no small part in these costs. In general, it's OK to spread property management costs throughout the year on a monthly basis, averaging the expenses. Once you are into the second year of renting, your forecasting will become more accurate as it will be based on actual costs recorded in the previous year.

If you are going to contract with a property management company that has an annual fee spread equally throughout the year — including contingencies such as checking for storm damage and regular security visits — you will be able to assign these as fixed costs. If, however, you intend to use the do-it-yourself method, more care needs to be taken in forecasting costs as many incidentals can be overlooked, leaving you out of pocket. For example, remember to include additional fuel costs incurred when traveling to and from the recreational property.

Insurance

Your household insurance policy may already cover you for rental for a few weeks of the year. If you plan to rent for more than that, check your coverage with your insurance company.

Marketing, promotion, and advertising

The forecast costs for marketing, promoting, and advertising your recreational property will depend on your decisions regarding marketing strategy and budget, and, of course, your decision about using a rental agency or not. If you have chosen to use a rental agency, you will not need to consider the costs of marketing, as that will be done for you. And if you have selected a rental agency that actively markets its properties out-of-season, you have no worries at all on this front. If you are going it alone, read Chapter 9, Marketing Your Vacation Home, which covers marketing in greater detail.

If you have chosen to do your own marketing, there will be up-front costs for a website, marketing literature, web advertising, and other promotion. Although you can allocate a figure for ad hoc advertising through the year, setting a marketing budget at the beginning of the year will help your bottom line and profit margin. Otherwise, it is all too easy to drift along month by month, registering here and there with different agencies and Internet advertisers, only to find you have overspent badly and received insufficient return on your marketing investment. Play with the figures in the Rental Calculator (on the CD-ROM) until you settle on a sensible figure for marketing. Then decide how best to spend that budget.

Contingency funds

Regardless of how meticulous you have been in estimating your overhead costs, there will probably be something you have overlooked, or some equipment failure or damage that requires additional funds. The amount you forecast for contingency funds depends on many factors, including the age of the property and when items such as water pumps, roofs, and appliances were last replaced. Then there is an element for sheer bad luck: Only you can judge how much to budget for that!

HOW MANY RENTAL WEEKS WILL YOU HAVE AVAILABLE?

Once you have a clear objective about how much income you want to generate, have set a realistic rental rate, and have accurately forecast the expenses, you will know the minimum number of weeks you'll need to rent to cover your expenses. Readers already involved in the financial aspects of a business will recognize this as identifying your breakeven point — the amount that you have to make in order to cover all your outgoing expenses. Once this has been defined and you have set a contingency amount to cover unexpected expenses, you can then forecast how much profit you will make.

The rental calculator and spreadsheets on the CD will let you calculate how many rental weeks you need to sell to pay all your expenses and perhaps cover some of your capital costs. Before you do this, think about your own and your family's use of the recreational property. To rent your cottage as a business rather than a hobby requires a commitment from the entire family, so once again, it's decision-making time!

When do you want to use the cottage for yourself and your family? Will you want several high-season weeks? What about Christmas/New Year's, public holidays, and school breaks? Unless you and your family are flexible enough to use the property only when it is vacant, you need to decide exactly what dates you have available for paying guests. Once the bookings start to come in, you won't be able to change your mind without seriously inconveniencing your clients, and possibly facing legal action.

To maximize your income, you'll need to rent during the entire summer, but that may not be practical if you have family who want to spend some time at your property. At times you may need to be strict with family and friends who may see your cottage as an inexpensive way to vacation, particularly if they have used it in this way in the past. Let everyone know that you are renting in a more professional manner, but that you may have late availability weeks or weekends that they can use. If you have minor jobs that need doing, you could save a little on property management by asking your nonpaying guests to do these tasks. Alternatively, have your nonpaying guests, family, or friends leave a gift for the cottage. Why not keep a list of items that may need replacing from time to time and ask nonpayers to choose from the list and take the replacement item with them to the cottage. Include things such as new pillows, towels, books and games, additions to the fishing tackle box, etc. Guests will appreciate knowing their gift is needed, and you will save on some of these expenses.

Jim Holland's Clear Lake cottage was a haven to many of his work friends, and he was happy for them to use the property when he wasn't spending time there himself. Once he started to rent seriously, he decided that he would offer time at the cottage if it hadn't been booked by the previous week. He left a "job jar" with a list of tasks that needed doing in a prominent position by the beer fridge (figuring this was the first place his guests would go!) with a note attached asking for at least one job to be done in return for the use of the cottage. From the notes of thanks in the guest book, everyone enjoyed the opportunity to give a little back.

Before deciding to rent your cottage in the winter season, give serious thought to what could possibly go wrong. For example, you will need someone to check the property very regularly when it is not occupied to make sure that the residual heating is working and pipes have not frozen. Offering winter rentals means ensuring you can guarantee a continuous supply of water, maintaining the heat throughout the season, and having snow removal organized so your guests can access the property without difficulty. These costs could be significant; however, if you are able to rent during Christmas and New Year's weeks, along with some rentals during January to March, winter rental could bring valuable income. However, if you are spending all your time troubleshooting winter problems for your guests, or worrying about what may happen, then maybe winter rentals are not such a good idea.

Having decided on the weeks you want to rent, you'll need to decide on your charging strategy. This is covered in the next chapter, What Is My Recreational Property Worth?

4
WHAT IS MY RECREATIONAL PROPERTY WORTH?

I recently asked a real estate friend how appraisers arrive at a figure for property valuation. After getting a short explanation of the principles of appraisal, I realized that setting a rate for a vacation rental week is not dissimilar.

What you will charge on a weekly basis for your property should be largely determined by what the market will bear, and this will depend on a number of criteria. Location (regional as well as physical), facilities offered, size, and ambience all play an important part, and it is well worthwhile spending time looking at comparable properties before making a decision. Regardless of whether you decide to go it alone and do your own marketing and advertising, or if you choose to use a rental agency, have a realistic idea of what rental fee you are expecting before you start planning. Doing the research now will pay dividends in the future as it will be a daunting task to make changes to your rental rates once you start advertising.

First of all, look at the websites of rental agencies servicing your area, then check local advertising sites. Finally, check out the larger sites where your potential competitors might advertise.

One way of setting a price is to decide whether you want to go the Wal-Mart route — high volume/low price — or the Chanel route — low volume/high price. However, setting rental rates is not an exact science; we will discuss different factors that will influence your pricing in this chapter

High-season rates are generally applicable from mid-June to early September, and for Christmas, New Year's, and the Spring break. Long weekends in the low-season period will generally attract higher rates. The rest of the year can be set at one rate, although if you are near a ski area, you might want to have an additional high-season or mid-season rate that covers the January to March period. Your location may dictate your seasons, so take a look at what your competitors are using for their low/mid/high-season dates.

LOCATION

Look for similar-sized recreational properties in your rental area. If your property is in a much-sought-after location, it may fetch a premium price. If it is a relatively short drive from a major city, rental rates can also be higher than in a more distant location. If your property has a unique selling point that may appeal to a particular section of the market, that could justify a higher price. For example, people looking for a peaceful, relaxing break will pay a premium if your vacation home is located on or near a no-motor lake. In locations that feature winter sports, properties that offer ski-in/out facilities will command a higher rate than those where additional driving is involved. In very popular tourist areas, vacation homes are more sought after than in quieter, less well-known locations.

If your property is located on good waterfront, this will clearly benefit your bookings in the summer months. However, if you are on or near a river offering canoe routes, you might expect additional bookings in spring and fall. Many European visitors, or those with young children, may prefer a swimming pool to open water, so if your property has a pool instead of (or even in addition to) waterfront, this could have a considerable impact on the potential rental value. Chapter 9, Marketing Your Vacation Home, will show just how you can boost your off-season income through reaching special interest groups with targeted packages and deals.

Interestingly, one Canadian rental agency infers on its website that cottages on rivers are virtually unrentable. However, as an owner of a riverside cottage myself, this is certainly not my experience. Indeed, visitors from the UK are happy to be near any water, despite the fact that no part of the UK is more than 112 kilometers from the sea! It is the fact that it can take three hours to get there (on a good day!) that prevents them from traveling, so water-based vacations of any type are what they are seeking. They don't bring boats so don't need marina or docking facilities, and, in general, demand less in terms of location than the home-grown Canadian market. So if you do have a charming riverside property, just find a more enlightened agency or adjust your marketing to target the guests who would find your home to be the right one for them.

SIZE

Most rental agencies would agree that larger properties tend to book up first for the high season and command higher prices. Many families or groups of friends like to vacation together, so a large vacation home sleeping ten people or more offers a more attractive and economical prospect than independently renting smaller properties. However, the market for smaller properties grows off-season when there are fewer families taking vacations. Rental guests in fall, winter, and spring will tend to be couples, either on their own, or two to three couples renting together. Whereas a large property sleeping eight to ten may achieve a high rent in the summer, it may remain largely empty in low season as the target audience at this time of year is unwilling to pay the price. A smaller, perhaps two-bedroom property, while yielding lower rents in high season, is more likely to rent additional weeks throughout the year. It's also worthwhile considering this if you are planning a renovation. Adding a sleeping cabin to offer additional summer sleeping space may be more cost-effective than spending a lot of money on additional bedrooms in the main residence.

Cottage owners Jan and Chas Clark have made the most of their renovated three-bedroom property and two-bedroom self-contained guest cottage. They find these facilities offer very flexible rental opportunities as both can be rented to larger parties in the summer, but either or both can be offered in out-of-season months, depending on demand.

AMENITIES

Location and size alone don't set the rental price: people will also expect certain levels of comfort and quality as the price rises. Yes, there are still a great many recreational homes across North America advertised as "basic and full of rustic charm" that fetch a bare minimum per week in high season. If you don't want to spend much time or money in making your property attractive to the higher spending market, you could easily achieve a reasonable return. However, if your goal is to make a substantial profit, you need to present your property in a way that will attract renters willing to pay a little more for that extra comfort and quality. Even a small property can command a good rent if it offers a high degree of ambience and comfort. Added features need not cost a large amount; the expense of refurbishment will pay off in the long run.

"We bought our lake cottage for $200,000 in September 2003. It was OK for rental — we could have just done a few minor alterations and it would have been ready to go and we could have easily got about $850–$900 per week in high season. However, we want to use it ourselves and it was in need of some loving attention. We ended up stripping it out, fitting a new kitchen and hardwood flooring, tiling the bathroom, redecorating throughout, and furnishing it with hard-wearing and durable materials. The total cost was just over $20,000 and we are now charging $1,350 per week — and this may turn out to be on the low side. It may take a couple of years to recoup the cost, but the value of the cottage has also increased by upgrading."

Think about how you can add value to your property. This could mean purchasing additional appliances, installing satellite TV and a DVD player, making sure the furniture and fittings are in good repair, etc. Purchasing attractive and matching furniture can require a considerable outlay but will reap rewards in the higher rental fee you can command. Offering air conditioning in summer and installing a good propane fireplace for winter warmth can both add significant value.

Think too about the décor. Grandma's hand-crocheted throw she made 40 years ago may have sentimental value and be quite functional over the old couch, but it won't go down well with the guests who have paid a premium price for their week's stay. Take a look around your property as if you were a renter about to pay $1,200 per week. What would you expect for that? Certainly not cracked and chipped dishes, or a 1970s-vintage single-channel television. You would expect the place to be well furnished, attractively decorated, and to have all the comforts of home. This attention to detail is all-important, and is explored further in Chapter 5, Getting Ready for Renting.

An inspector for a rental agency recalls arriving at a property one late May afternoon to value the property for inclusion in the agency's portfolio. He reports:

"The outside of the cottage was just gorgeous — lawns leading down to sparkling water, flower tubs on the deck — I just had great feelings about it. Then I went inside. What a letdown that was, although it could have been so different. There was cherry wood flooring, cedar and pine surrounds, with huge picture windows overlooking the lake. But the furniture was ancient and mildewed, the appliances looked like they were out of the ark, and a very unpleasant smell pervaded every room. The owner seemed unaware that there was anything unusual about this and chatted about how much he could make on rental. He was already renting ad hoc to friends for $1,000 per week, but was hoping to achieve more through our agency. My report was clear: If he was willing to upgrade throughout, have the place thoroughly cleaned, and employ a service to undertake rental turnarounds, he could expect to increase his rental income by as much as 75 percent. Outlay on the upgrades and maintenance would be recouped over the first summer."

If your property is on the waterfront, what watercraft are you prepared to offer to guests? The minimum should be a canoe or pedal boat, although some owners offer a rowboat, sailboat, or windsurfer. Allowing your guests the use of a boat with a motor is not recommended as this has greater inherent risks and subsequently higher insurance premiums. In general, it is far better to have details about the local marina, with daily and weekly rental rates.

Do you have launching facilities for guests' own boats? Is there a marina or public boat launch nearby? Are there bicycles available for guest use? Do you have a pool/billiard table? All of these features add value and help your cottage to stand out in an overcrowded off-season market.

For year-round rental, think about the attractiveness of fall and winter vacations at your cottage. Is there a wood-burning stove, a Jacuzzi, perhaps a hot tub? Satellite TV is definitely an attraction for out-of-season guests, so it is worth the cost of installing it. Some owners of cottages attracting quality renters offer computer and modem connection for those who need to be in constant contact with their office. If you are in an area with high-speed Internet connection, there is distinct added value in offering this. Remember that providing these additional amenities may incur maintenance costs that must be allowed for in your calculations. The overhead for keeping a hot tub going throughout the winter, for instance, can be high, so your winter rental rate should reflect this. Owners in ski areas charge more for their vacation rentals in the winter than in summer — and their occupancy rates are higher! Just remember that higher prices equal higher expectations. If you intend to charge executive rates, you must provide executive facilities to match.

WILL IT RENT AS IT IS?

A good starting point to gauge how well your property will rent is to do an analysis of the good and the bad points, the opportunities you have available to rent, and the problems you may face along the way. This is known as a SWOT (Strengths, Weaknesses, Opportunities, and Threats) summary and is a useful way to determine what is unique about your property. In this analysis, what may devalue your property are its weaknesses, and the obstacles you may have to overcome in order to maximize your investment are the threats.

Sample 2 is an example of a SWOT analysis.

MAKING CHANGES

Once you have done this analysis, you are able to look objectively at what you will have to do to shore up the weaknesses and challenge the threats. In this example, you may decide on the following changes:

- Improve the amenities you offer to put your property at a higher rental level than your local competition. For example, purchasing a hot tub pays dividends in increased bookings in the colder months. Providing a computer and Internet access will also give you that competitive edge.

SAMPLE 2
SWOT ANALYSIS

Strengths	Opportunities
• Modern kitchen with dishwasher • Well-furnished throughout • South-facing aspect • Cozy ambience for winter	• Great hiking area • Many tourist attractions close by • Main snowmobile trail runs near property • Year-round activities
Weaknesses	**Threats**
• Lots of competition with many other rental properties in the area • Access in winter can be challenging • No laundry facilities	• Other local properties rent quite cheaply • Local rental agency has lots of cottages empty during the off-season

- Promote the advantages to specialist hiking/walking groups for fall and spring, and to snowmobile enthusiasts during winter. Offer special packages such as "Breakfast included" (where you stock the fridge with breakfast fixings).

- Explore ways of making the property more winter-accessible and for attracting people looking for a winter getaway.

- Develop one-year, three-year, and five-year plans that incorporate prioritized capital improvements.

- Purchase a combination washer/dryer that will fit into a small space.

Use the SWOT analysis form on the CD to do your own summary.

If you are using an agency, let them know you plan to add value by making changes, and make sure these are mentioned on their web pages. If you have chosen your agency carefully, they will be actively promoting out-of-season rentals and will welcome discussion on how best to market your property.

CALCULATING THE BOTTOM LINE

Once you have your targets set, know how many weeks you have available for rental, have analyzed the current status of your cottage, and planned for improvements, you can then decide on the level of flexibility you have for late availability and off-season bookings.

If you have planned your marketing strategy well, you should never need to make price reductions during high season. As long as demand remains high and the number of properties available to rent is limited, you will rent throughout the summer, providing your pricing is realistic. Being more flexible with your rates becomes more important at other times of the year when your potential guests may be more sensitive to higher prices. Keep an eye on what other owners are doing by checking constantly on the competition.

Input your own figures into the working rental calculator on the CD to get a more accurate assessment. Sample 3 is based on figures for the lake cottage mentioned earlier in this chapter.

With the total monthly expense figure calculated, you can then divide that by your proposed weekly rental rate. From the result, you will see how many weeks you will need to rent to break even. Now add in the number of weeks you can realistically expect to rent to arrive at the net profit you can reasonably expect to make. With a high-season rental rate of $1,400, this cottage needs to be rented for 12 weeks to pay the mortgage and monthly overheads, which is a realistic expectation.

SAMPLE 3
RENTAL CALCULATOR

Breakdown of costs	$
Purchase price	200,000
Down payment	75,000
Mortgage	125,000
CASH REQUIRED	$
Down payment	75,000
Furniture, fixtures/fittings	20,000
Closing costs	8,000
Total cash needed	103,000
MONTHLY EXPENSES	$
Mortgage	
Principal & interest @ 5% over 20 years	825
Monthly overhead	
Insurance (building & contents)	60
Heating & lighting	200
Telephone	35
Security system monitoring	25
Satellite TV subscription (basic tariff)	35
Grounds maintenance & snowplowing	100
Property management fee	110
Total monthly expenses	1,390

5
GETTING READY FOR RENTING

While doing research for this book I spoke with many owners of recreational homes, some who had owned their properties for years and many who had bought in more recent years for investment purposes. Their collective experiences gave a consistent message: Get it right from the start and the process, although not always smooth, will be easier.

A great example came from a couple who bought a lovely property on outstanding waterfront. It was well decorated throughout, with good kitchen and bathroom fittings. With it came a three-bedroom guest house which was more of a basic cottage. The previous owners had left it furnished as they had rented it in the past. The furnishings were basic, unmatched, and generally tired; the appliances were elderly and had definitely seen better days, while the pictures on the walls would not sell at a yard sale. It might have been tempting to leave it as it was: the two homes could be rented together as a large property, with the smaller one being marketed as overflow accommodation. However, the owners took an objective view of how they wanted to market it and decided that they wanted to attract large families or two families who wanted to vacation together. With this in mind, they didn't want the guest house to be seen as second best. They decided to strip it out, redecorate, and bring it up to the standard of the main house. The results spoke for themselves with return renters, and created an opportunity to rent the guest house on its own in the winter at a much higher weekly rate.

GETTING IT RIGHT FROM THE START

If you have already been renting your vacation home for many years you might be wondering what you can learn from this book that you don't already know. However, since you picked it up and have read as far as this chapter, you may want to make more money from your property than you do at present. Perhaps you need to take a fresh look at what you are offering your guests for their money. For example, consider the furnishings and appliances, the contents of your kitchen cupboards, toys and games, outdoor equipment, and the general ambience of your property.

"We were so excited about the house we'd rented. We'd booked it over the Internet directly from the owner. He was enthusiastic about it over the phone, and the pictures on his website gave a great impression. We flew out from the UK the day before and stayed in Toronto for the first night. The following day, we did our grocery shopping and arrived at the appointed time to meet the owner. It was disastrous. He had been there for a few days, clearly having quite a good time with friends, and was still cleaning up. The place smelled of stale beer, cigarette smoke, and wet dog (he had a large dog that seemed to spend most of its time, when not in the lake, on the white couch!). He still had a few hours' cleaning to do, but we decided (seeing his general state) that it would be quicker to do it ourselves, and he went weaving on his way. When we explored the cottage — which could have been lovely — we found it was dirty and uncared for. There was filth under the beds (and a pair of men's underpants!), the windows were so dirty they had to be washed to get a reasonable view of the lake, the bath was grimy, and the bedding we had expected was thread-bare and had holes. Fortunately, we had friends living locally who helped us out with bedding and came out to help us clean. In the end, we made the most of it and had a good vacation, but we would never go back nor recommend it to others. Although we left it in a tidy state, and probably the cleanest it had been for many years, we just felt sorry for the people arriving next as I'm sure they would have been disappointed too."

This story is a shameful example and shows a sloppy, uncaring approach that stems from high demand for properties in that location and a corresponding limited supply in the high season. It's an extreme example — one that would merit a prime slot in a TV program titled *Vacations from Hell!*

"It was a nice place and it was great outside, but the inside just looked a little tired and worn — we wouldn't go back."

"What a shame the owner hadn't paid attention to the inside of the cottage. The shower was scaled up and we had to clean it before it was worth using."

"The microwave was broken, the barbecue filthy. If anyone had checked the place after the last people left, they would have found this out. It was obvious nobody had checked it."

These are just a few of the comments I received during the research for this book. This isn't the kind of feedback you'll be looking for, as these guests won't come back. But with a little effort, and without huge expense, you can create a look that shows you care.

PROPERTY AUDIT

Doing a thorough audit can reveal all sorts of deficiencies that you might not have previously considered, and indeed may not feel are worth changing, either in terms of cost or time. This is a critical exercise, so it's probably best not to do it on a lovely warm day when the sun is sparkling on the water, the happy sound of children playing fills the air, and the barbecue is sending out wafts of mouth-watering aromas. Instead, carry out a systematic analysis of your property on a cool, cloudy day, when your judgment won't be influenced by the beauty of the surroundings.

If you have just bought or are intending to buy a vacation home for rental, do this audit at the start. Start by putting yourself in potential renters' shoes, and build a wish list for a wonderful vacation in this property. Then, go through the home room by room and make a further list of items needed to fulfill the wish list. Use the Cost of Furnishings Worksheet provided on the CD to calculate costs for each room. Sample 4 shows the cost of all new furnishings for a three-bedroom property. If you furnish with durable fixtures and fittings that will stand the test of time and a multitude of renters, your furnishings should stay smart and clean with minimal effort.

FURNISHINGS AND APPLIANCES

If your goal is to create a great first impression for your guests, look carefully at your furniture and appliances. If you are furnishing an unfurnished property, don't be tempted to scour yard sales and the small ads in the local paper for used furniture and appliances — unless you are prepared to spend time renovating, painting, and polishing. It's no fun bringing that bargain bed to the cottage, setting it up in the bedroom and finding a distinctly unpleasant smell coming from the mattress when the heating is turned up!

To furnish for professional renting, go to a reputable discount furniture store and make a deal with them to supply you with a houseful of furniture at a good discount. Take a look at the Cottage Furnishing Sample on the CD, which gives a good indication of the average cost for furnishing a recreational property.

SAMPLE 4
COST OF FURNISHINGS

Living room	$	Kitchen	$
Couches @ $600	1,200	Kettle	35
End tables @ $125	250	Coffeemaker	35
Coffee table	160	Microwave oven	100
TV & stereo stand	300	Storage jars	45
Rugs @ $100	200	Knives/utensils	75
Bookcase	150	Cutlery	80
Lamps @ $60	180	Crockery	70
TV/video/stereo	600	Pots and Pans	130
Chair	150	Casserole dishes	40
Miscellaneous items	300	Glassware	60
Total	**3,490**	Miscellaneous items	300
		Total	**970**
Dining room		**Cleaning**	
Table/chairs x 8	1,200	Washer/dryer	700
Table coverings, etc.	100	Vacuum	200
Total	**1,300**	Iron and board	60
		Miscellaneous items	100
		Total	**1,060**
Bedroom 1		**Bedroom 3**	
Queen bed set	650	Double hb/base	175
Side tables @ $100	200	Double mattress	250
Chest/dressing table	300	Dresser	150
Bedding	250	Bedding	200
Miscellaneous items	100	Side tables @ $100	200
Total	**1,500**	Miscellaneous items	100
		Total	**1,075**
Bedroom 2		**Outside**	
Single hb/base x 2	350	Canoe	500
Single mattresses x 2	300	Life jackets	180
Bedding	175	Toys	200
Side table	100	Miscellaneous garden items	200
Dresser	150	**Total**	**1,080**
Miscellaneous items	100		
Total	**1,175**		
		Grand total	**11,650**

It is quite tempting to go for the lower price bracket for your recreational home setup, and in some cases that is fine. Inexpensive kitchenware may be all that you need providing you have replacements, as some things will get broken. In fact, it's a good idea to spend as little as possible on glass and dishware for this reason. However, it is a false economy to go for the cheapest furniture, as the following story illustrates.

"We bought the house for our own use for a couple of weeks a year, but mostly as an investment, using the rental income to pay the expenses. If I were to do this again, there are quite a few things I'd do differently. For a start, I bought a new stove — the cheapest one in the store. After a whole summer of paying my cleaner extra hours, I realized I could have saved by spending a little more on a self-cleaning model — even a used one from a good dealer. I also got the cheapest deck furniture possible, which had to be thrown out after the end of the season. Next time, I'll look at paying a bit more but saving on replacement costs. And, of course, the higher quality stuff gives the place a better look overall, which might mean another $50 or more a week extra in income. And we enjoy it more because the cottage looks more like a home than a 'rental.'"

A typical rental property can look bland, and it is well worth the effort to give it a more lived-in look. If you are purchasing a recreational property simply for rental, and to perhaps use yourself for a couple of weeks per year, think about how to make it look like a home rather than a rental unit. Hang good pictures rather than bland landscapes, maybe with a theme for each room. Buy a few ornaments, candlesticks, and other decorative items, maybe some dried flower arrangements or good quality artificial plants — anything that makes it look cared for and loved. It is too easy to create a sterile environment because it is "just a rental" and you don't want to spend too much on it. But remember you should be aiming for that "Wow" reaction — that first impression as your guests walk in the door. Ask yourself, "What wows me?"

"The cottage we stayed in was really big, lots of space and room for all of us. But it felt so empty and it echoed. It really lacked character, which was a shame as the location was fabulous."

Bedding

Whether or not you will supply bedding for your guests is a decision you will need to make. This is often dictated by the accepted standard for your location. For instance, in Ontario "cottage country," it is generally expected that guests will bring their own linens, so many owners simply supply pillows and blankets. In many other North American locations, it is expected that bedding and towels will be provided.

Not supplying linens rules out the opportunity to rent to international visitors, who will not have sufficient baggage allowance to make bringing their own linens a feasible option. In addition, transatlantic guests are likely to arrive very late in the evening after a long flight, and with a five- to six-hour time difference will be extremely tired. To then have to make up beds can create a negative first impression, which should be avoided if you want to have satisfied guests. If you want to attract international guests you will need to supply linens and have the beds made. In addition, consider guests who are staying for more than one week and will need sufficient linens to allow a weekly change, especially if you do not have laundry facilities on site.

If you use a property management company or rental agency, check with them to see whether they offer a bed-making service. You can then leave a good supply of linens for changeovers and be confident that it will be done for your next guests. Some agencies will also provide linens, but make sure the quality is good and the colors coordinate appropriately. If you are presenting your property at its best, you will want to make sure that the presentation isn't spoiled by threadbare sheets and faded comforters.

If you decide you'll provide comforters and ask your guests to bring their own sheets, think about the hygiene aspect of this.

"We rented a beautiful home last summer and it was fine in all respects apart from the linens. We'd asked if there would be linens supplied and were told we only needed to bring sheets and pillow covers. When we arrived and went to make up the beds, I noticed a really bad smell from the comforter on the bed in the master bedroom. It was covered in dog hair and didn't look or smell as though it had been washed all summer. All the other beds were the same. The one in the kids' bedroom was even worse! We had to use them the first night as it was late — then washed them all the following day. It was a good thing there was a washer/dryer or we would have been really stuck."

— *A rental guest from Scotland*

If you are buying new bedding, consider good quality duvets (comforters), each with two sets of duvet covers. This way, when you do the changeover, you can slip one cover off, the other on, and take the laundry home. Buying duvets is a bit of an expense at the outset but worth it in the long run as they do tend to last longer and are more hard wearing. Supply an attractive bed cover and pillow shams and the bedrooms will look great. Some of the best rental property bedrooms I have seen would not have been out of place in a top-quality bed-and-breakfast establishment; they attract higher rentals and plenty of returning guests.

Resist the temptation to use older linens that you might have had for some time at home, and don't be tempted to skimp and buy inferior linens — this is a false economy. You will want to launder comforters, and some of the cheap ones don't last the first wash, let alone several over the course of a few rental weeks. Look at it as if you were running a bed-and-breakfast, but without being there to provide the breakfast. Guests would not expect to make up their own beds, nor would they expect threadbare sheets and comforters. Going the extra mile here is definitely important, and will pay dividends in the long run.

The same goes for towels. Provide high-quality indoor towels and they will last longer and definitely look better. Also provide a pile of fresh outdoor towels for your guests. These are not expensive and make such a difference.

Provide each bed with a good quality mattress and pillow covers. These are really worth the investment, and should be checked frequently for stains and wear and tear. Waterproof mattress covers for children's beds will provide added peace of mind for you, but please don't put plastic padded mattress covers on the main bed.

> "We booked this great house for our 25th wedding anniversary and just loved every aspect of it ... except the plastic-coated mattress cover! It was so uncomfortable that we removed it after the second night, which left a bare mattress that was equally uncomfortable even with the sheets on top. Why do owners do this?"
>
> — *A guest in a vacation home in Sedona, AZ*

Linen items can be added to your list of "house needs" that you'll give to your family and friends. Then, when they come to stay, they can donate some new towels, pillows, or mattress covers. Or you may decide you just don't want to go to the expense of providing linens. Whatever your decision, take an objective look at what you are providing and make sure it is of a standard that reflects your rental rate.

PERSONAL ITEMS

I know of rental properties that the owners and their families use regularly on long weekends and during some high-season weeks, as well as having plenty of trips up in the shoulder season. This may well be what you plan to do: After all, this is your piece of heaven and you want to experience it as often as you can.

Naturally, you'll want to make it a home-away-from-home, but it is important that you balance this against how much you want your renters to know about you. Should you cover the walls with family photos, keep your cottage clothes in the wardrobe and drawers, leave all your food in the kitchen cupboard, fridge, and freezer, pile magazines and children's toys in a basket in the family room?

Of course you can do this, but you need to put yourself in your guests' shoes and think about the impression your family's clutter may give.

For a moment, think of yourself as the person who has just arrived at your cottage after a long drive. You've paid your rental fee and have great expectations of the property based on the description and photographs you've been sent or have seen on a website. For the time you are there, you want to feel it's your own vacation home, your own pride and joy. This fantasy is a little difficult to envisage, though, if you open drawers to find someone else's personal things, and the fridge is full of half-empty jars of pickles and margarine tubs.

You can easily balance your need to feel the recreational property is your own with a good understanding of the needs of your paying guests. It requires a little planning, but will make a big difference to renters — and keep them coming back again and again.

"For our cottage we found a portable plastic 'cupboard' with shelves and hangers, and bought a couple of good-sized plastic boxes with lids that we keep in the basement. One box holds nonperishable food items — tins, packets, bottles, and jars; another contains clothes; a third is packed with personal items from the bathroom cabinet, etc. Shelves hold books and games we don't want guests to use (we have a lovely backgammon set that has been handed down through the family for generations and is really treasured). We also have a box that keeps our family photos so when we arrive for weekends or longer stays, we just take down the landscapes and prints and replace them with family snaps. Within half an hour after we arrive, we've transformed the cottage back to our own personal space."

WHAT TO SUPPLY?

Owners often ask me how far they should go in supplying basic items. Should they leave out just one roll of toilet paper per bathroom, or make sure there is a supply for the duration of the rental?

Should they provide coffee, tea, sugar, foil, cling wrap, etc? There are several schools of thought here —

- to supply all the standard items guests will need for the duration of their stay,

- to supply the basics to tide them over for the first day or two, or

- to provide nothing

The third option seems a little harsh, particularly if your guests have come a long way and may arrive late. Leaving at least the basics is a nice gesture that they will appreciate. If you decide to supply a good range of standard items, keep a checklist to make sure they are topped up between rentals.

Whatever option you choose, make sure your guests know in advance what they will need to bring with them. A list accompanying the final payment confirmation will give them enough time to plan the things they will need. If you are going to leave staple items, let your guests know there will be supplies they can use.

"We have had guests complain that food was left in the fridge by the previous guests and they had to throw it away. It was in fact ketchup, mustard, relish, a jar of peanut butter, maple syrup, and salad dressing. All of these were nearly full so we had decided to leave them for the next guests to use. They obviously didn't like that idea, as they made it known to us! We have since made a point of including a section in our guest guide to say there may be basic food items left, and if they don't want to use them, don't. These items can go to the back of the fridge, or our property manager can remove them if some guests really don't want them. We also ask that if guests do use food staples, that they please replace them before they leave. This seems to work on most occasions."

Based on my research and interviews with property owners, there are no hard-and-fast rules about food staples. It seems that whatever you choose to do, there will be guests happy with it, and some who just aren't. Clear advice in your guest guide will alert your guests to your policy on what is available for their use. One owner I spoke with advises that guests can use the freezer, but should not touch the food in the marked bags, as this belongs to him. He says this works well — it gives guests an additional food storage option, and he has never experienced any of his own frozen foods going missing.

"Once when we were rushing back to the city, we left our own food in the freezer section of the fridge in the cottage kitchen: two cowboy steaks, some chili, and a tub of ice cream. When the next guests had left and we went up to inspect and do some work on the property, we noticed a really bad smell in the laundry room. When we opened the old freezer in the laundry room, we discovered the smell came from our wizened and rotting steaks. The guests had decided to move our food out, but didn't notice that the freezer was actually switched off!"

Leave a good supply of cleaning materials, otherwise you can't expect your guests to do a good job of cleaning before they leave (if that is what you expect them to do). If you are supplying linens and ask your guests to start the laundry on the day they leave, make sure there is plenty of detergent available. One owner uses a "new season starter" list. On it, she lists all the supplies and where they are kept (see Sample 5).

The owner uses this list when the cottage is opened up for the summer and also checks the items off the list at each changeover. If you contract with someone to take care of your property in your absence, you can provide them with checklists for replacing supplies. The CD has examples of checklists that you can adapt to your own needs.

TOYS, BOOKS, AND GAMES

It's a great idea to have a selection of games and toys that your guests can use, but be aware that they may not treat them with the same respect you would expect from your own family. This is not

LIST OF SUPPLIES

Washroom	3 rolls toilet paper
	Hand soap
	Toilet cleaner
	2 bath towels, 2 hand towels
Bedroom 1	Flashlight in bedside drawers (check batteries)
	Box of tissues
Kitchen	Garbage bags
	Coffee filters
	Paper towels
	Tea towels
	Foil splash guards/oven tray
	Tinfoil
	Cling wrap

to say they won't be looked after, but there is the risk toys will be broken and pieces from games will go astray. If you have treasured family games, it's probably best to put these in your owner's cupboard when you are not there and to supply a selection of other games for guest use only. Yard sales and flea markets can provide a good supply and, as long as the games are all complete, it is quite acceptable to fill your games box with used games.

If you provide toys, make sure they comply with safety regulations and are in good condition. It would be sad if guests had to sign a disclaimer to say you are not responsible for any injury their children might suffer through playing with toys you have provided, but in these litigious times this may not be long in coming. A little care is needed to balance the desire to add value with sensible caution by supplying a small range of toys and games that are clean and fit for use. After each rental, check the toy box, remove any damaged items, and wash or wipe down the rest.

People love to play cards when they are at the cottage so it's a nice touch to supply a couple of packs. These aren't expensive, so do change them when they get sticky or grubby. It's no fun playing a fast game of euchre when the cards are sticking together. Checking the cards are all there and the games are intact should be part of your changeover routine. If you are getting ready for renting and are making a games collection for the first time, the following are some suggested items to include:

- Crib board — Make sure there are pegs with the board
- Connect Four
- Scrabble — Check that all the letters are there!
- Trivial Pursuit
- Clue
- Monopoly
- Colored pencils/pencil sharpener
- Books of card games or instructions on how to play your favorite ones

If you are going to supply a selection of paperback books, include a note in your guest guide advising guests whether they can remove them or not. It's a nice gesture to say they may take away a book they are reading, as long as they leave one they have finished in its place. I have found that my cottage libraries keep growing as guests tend to leave more than they take away! However, if you have books you definitely want to keep, mark something similar to the following clearly on the inside cover:

> Property of this library.
> This book belongs to the Bayer family.
> Please don't take it away.

Put a selection of children's books in the smaller bedrooms, perhaps with some coloring books and a pot of crayons, making sure they are not wax crayons. We've seen the results when children have taken wax crayons to cottage walls — the scribbling is very difficult to clean!

If your property regularly has wildlife — beavers, deer, raccoons, hummingbirds, etc. — think about putting together an activity pack for children so they can spot animals and birds and mark them on a sheet. All these little extras add to the value you are giving your guests and will help your rental property stand out from the rest.

Guidebooks and maps

Many guests will have done their homework before they come and will have a range of maps and guides with them. However, there will also be a large number who have no idea what your local area offers and will be expecting some guidance. You're the expert on this, so share your knowledge with them. If you know where the best hiking trails are, which part of the lake is best for fishing, and the good places to stop on a snowmobile outing, write a few lines about each activity. Keep a folder of this information, together with leaflets on places to go and things to do in the area, and add these to a section at the back of your cottage guide. If you have room, maybe in a family room or hallway, put up a corkboard and pin a good map of the area with local places of interest and restaurants.

If you have guidebooks, clearly mark them with the property name and a polite request that they are not taken away. Think about the differing interests your guests might have and supply guides accordingly. Check your local bookstore for books on your locality and areas of interest. Maps of canoe routes, hiking trails, cross-country ski guides, and where to find ghost towns are all of potential interest. If you want to attract winter guests, contact your local snowmobile association and get a collection of trail maps; if in a ski region, provide plenty of information on the best slopes, ski schools, and après ski venues. Contact the office at the closest ski resort to see if you can negotiate a discount on ski passes or ski lessons for your guests as an incentive for them to book with you. The tourist offices for your region will have a lot of information on events and activities in your area. Just remember to keep the brochures up to date. Your guests will really appreciate comprehensive and current information, including restaurant recommendations and open hours.

If you are in an area where there is an abundance of information about local activities, separate the brochures into different clearly marked folders. Alternatively, you can purchase a small wall-mounted leaflet rack from an office supplies store. Categories for sorting the information could include the following:

- Hiking trails
- Things to do on rainy days
- Outings for small children
- Eating out
- Renting bicycles, snowmobiles, boats

Anglers will want to know where the nearest bait store is and will welcome any information about the best spots on the lake to head for. If your recreational property is on a large lake, have a good lake map available and leave a selection of pins and sticky notes so guests can offer their own recommendations for good places to fish.

"Our home has a picture board that we started with our own 'best catch' pictures. After a summer of renting, we found that our guests were adding their own photos, and then they began sending them to us to put on the board. It looks great and our guests often mention it in the visitors' book."

ADDING VALUE

By far the best and cheapest way of marketing your vacation home is through word of mouth. If your guests have had a great time, they will tell other people. They will also want to come back, and not only in the high-season months. When they see your low-season rates, they may also book weekends in the off seasons, when you really want to increase your rental income. Remember that first impressions count for so much. Here are a few ideas to add that little bit extra that can turn a pleasant stay into a truly memorable one:

- *Leave a bottle of wine to greet guests on arrival.* If you are in a wine-growing region, a bottle from a smaller winery can be an unusual and welcome gift.

- *Offer a get-you-settled grocery shopping service for overseas visitors or those traveling long distances.* Ask them to email or fax their grocery list and arrange to have the groceries delivered to the property before your guests arrive. Add in a little something extra — maybe a local delicacy, as a small gift.

- *Leave a welcome note letting guests know when you (or your representative) will be over to see them.* Don't use the note to add in any last minute instructions — that would alter the spirit of the message.

- *In winter, light the wood stove or fireplace in enough time before your guests' arrival to create a welcoming ambience.*

- *If your guests are a couple on a romantic weekend, put out fresh candles and dim the lighting.* Find a classical or easy-listening station on the radio, and leave it on as background music.

"Staying in a Cornwall (England) cottage last year, we were delighted to find a welcome note, together with a home-baked cake — it was such a lovely touch. The note included brief details of a concert that was on locally the next day. If they hadn't let us know, we would have missed it."

SPECIAL OCCASIONS
Christmas, New Year's, and other festive occasions

Renting your property for the festive season means that you are providing the venue for your guests to enjoy their own celebrations in the comfort of your vacation home. It is perhaps an opportunity for families to celebrate together in a larger venue, or for a change of environment. You will undoubtedly be charging a premium for this, so you need to go that extra mile to create a festive atmosphere. An undecorated cottage can take on a lonely, dreary feel the week before Christmas, so even if your guests tell you they would like to decorate for themselves, make sure you have added your own touch of festivity. For added value, ask them if they would like a real tree or an artificial one — and whether they would like you to trim it — and add decorative touches around the cottage.

Theme weekends

If you are marketing weekends based on themes of local festivals or events — such as music festivals or lobster festivals — have a basket containing tourist leaflets or other kinds of information that relate to the events. Include any discount coupons that local businesses may be offering. (See Chapter 9, Marketing Your Vacation Home, for more ideas about using this type of promotion to increase occupancy.)

6
EMERGENCIES AND CONTINGENCIES

Being prepared for emergencies doesn't mean thinking of every conceivable disaster that may befall your property or guests and then worrying for the duration of every rental in case one of them happens. It simply means you make sure you provide emergency information as clearly and concisely as you can. The following story illustrates what can happen when a seemingly minor piece of information is omitted. When this story was first related our reaction was, "Can people really be that dumb?" On reflection, it was a great example of what happens when instructions are not as clear as they could be.

"A colleague of mine, together with numerous far-flung friends, recently decided to rent a remote cottage for a reunion weekend to take advantage of the fall colors and to celebrate the significant birthday of one of the group.

"The various members of the group traveled independently and arrived at the cottage around noon — and the beer and wine started to flow. During the course of the afternoon the weather began to deteriorate, with very strong winds and driving rain, and it came as no surprise when the power failed. Undeterred, the group continued to party, and as evening descended a solitary candle was found and lit. The winds grew stronger and the group was suddenly startled by a huge crash outside the cottage. Investigating the source of the noise, they found that a large tree branch had come down, narrowly missing the cottage and the vehicles parked outside. However, the tree had also brought down the power line to the cottage.

"After some discussion, and the discovery that there was a complete absence of cell phone signal, it was agreed that two of the group would drive the 30 minutes to the nearest town to phone the power company and report the damage to the line. By the time they reached the small town, having had to dodge other fallen trees along the way, it was around nine o'clock. The streets were deserted, and the wind and rain battered the phone booth on the corner of the street. The power company was contacted and after pushing all the right buttons, as directed by the robotic automated help line, my colleague was eventually connected to a human being. 'What is the address and meter number of the property?' the robot asked.

"Aaarggghhh! Needless to say this was not information that was readily available, which ended the telephone conversation there and then. By now, the party atmosphere had definitely begun to fade and the 30-minute journey back to the cottage seemed endless. The group spent the next 45 minutes with fading torches searching for the electricity meter, which was eventually discovered behind a carefully camouflaged door on the outside of the property.

"Armed with the vital information, the intrepid pair set off once again for the remote town, filed the damage report, and returned to the cottage just before midnight. The party restarted but was somewhat subdued as there was no way to cook the meal that had been brought for that evening, and the trek to the lake for water to flush the toilet was becoming longer and longer. However, a little later the group was somewhat shocked to hear a telephone ringing in the cottage and after some frantic scrabbling found the phone fixed to a wall behind the kitchen door. Surprise, surprise — it was the power company calling to inform them that the line damage should be fixed first thing in the morning. Needless to say, there were red faces all round on realizing there had been a phone available in the cottage all the time!"

When people are out of their familiar home environment and, even worse, in a different country, even a minor emergency can induce a state of panic. Property owners may see power outages as a nuisance — something they are used to — whereas an unexpected power cut could cause a real challenge for people unfamiliar with the way systems work in more remote recreational homes. Making clear what should be done in case of any emergency is really important and it requires a lot of thought to cover every eventuality.

Ghoulish though it might seem, a family brainstorming session on what might go wrong can often produce a wealth of nasty scenarios and will allow you to provide enough information in the emergency section of the guest guide to deal with most situations. Start with drawing a line down a sheet of paper, list all the potential disasters in the left-hand column and in the right column write a brief list of the sequence of events your guests should follow.

THE EMERGENCY SECTION OF YOUR GUEST GUIDE

The guest guide should include a special section entitled "What to do in an emergency." Encourage guests to read this section by mentioning it in boldface type in the guide's introduction:

IMPORTANT: MAKE SURE YOU READ THE SECTION ON EMERGENCIES ON PAGE 10

You can't be there to make sure it is read, but at least you have made every effort to direct attention to the information you have provided.

Answers to the following questions will be the basis of the emergency section in your guest guide. (Use the Emergency Preparedness Worksheet on the CD to prepare your answers.)

Medical/fire emergencies

- If there is no phone at the property, where is the nearest phone booth?

- Is there a cell phone signal?

- What are the emergency telephone numbers in your area?

- To enable the emergency services to find the property, what is the 911 or legal description of the property?

- What is the expected reaction time of emergency services?

- Who should they expect to arrive? (In some rural areas, a "First Response" vehicle may be dispatched from the local fire hall. This will carry equipment to allow for basic first aid to be administered until an ambulance arrives. Check with your municipal office for information on what to include in your guide.)

- How far is it to the nearest hospital?

- Where is the nearest walk-in clinic?

- Where is the first aid kit in the cottage?

- Who replenishes the first aid kit in the cottage?

- How will you know if the first aid kit has been used?

- Where are the fire extinguisher and fire blankets stored?

- Are a hose pipe and outdoor faucet available? Where are they?

- When did you last test the smoke alarms?

System breakdowns

- Who do your guests call in the event of a failure or emergency with any systems — you or your representative? (If your property is managed by a rental agency, there may be a particular procedure your guests follow according to the arrangement you have with the agency.)

- For reporting power outages, what is the property's legal description, account name/number, and meter number?

- To enable the contractor/utility company to find the property, what is the 911 or legal description of the property?

- What is the expected reaction time for each contractor?

- Are your chosen contractors aware that they are "on call" for your clients?

- Are your chosen contractors familiar with the property's location and the equipment/service they may be called out to deal with?

- How will payment to the contractor be handled?

- Where is the breaker panel located and is each breaker accurately and legibly described? (Mark the important breakers with colored tape, e.g., red for water heater and blue for water pump. Refer to this in the section "what to do in an emergency" in your guest guide.)

- Where is the valve to turn off the water?

- How is the water pump isolated?

- Is there a heated line? How is it controlled?

- Where is the septic emptying point? (This must be accurately described and/or physically marked so it can be located easily under snow, for example.)

- What should the guests do if a critical appliance (stove, fridge, toaster, kettle, coffee machine, TV, stereo) breaks down?

- What alternative heating systems are available in the event of a lengthy power outage in winter?

Power outage kit

If you have been at your property during a power outage you'll know what you need to have at hand. Because you are familiar with the cottage layout and know where everything is kept, it's relatively easy to find a flashlight, candles, a radio, etc. But remember that your guests may have just arrived on a cold and snowy night. It's pitch black outside, and they have no idea where to find anything. Having an emergency box available for guests in the event of the power going out may prevent unwanted and unnecessary calls, so it's worthwhile taking the time to put one together. The following are some basic items to include in your power outage kit:

- Powerful lantern-type flashlight (and separate battery)

- Box containing half a dozen candles and a box of matches (make sure you also have candleholders)

- One or two oil lamps together with a bottle of (indoor) lamp oil

- Sealed 5-liter container of fresh drinking water

- Small, cheap battery-powered radio (keep batteries in a separate container)

- First aid kit

- Laminated card with emergency numbers and other priority information such as local radio frequency

Your guests need to know where the power outage kit is, so include clear instructions in the guest guide on where to find it, and display this prominently. Some examples of instructions include the following:

If the power goes off, there is a large flashlight on top of the fridge and small ones in each bedside drawer. Emergency numbers are listed at the end of this guide. We have also provided an emergency kit for use only in the event of an extended power outage. The kit contains an additional first aid box, water, candles, flashlight, oil lamps, and a battery radio. There is also a card listing the numbers to call and the information to give the power company when reporting an outage.

Candles and oil lamps are to be used only under strict adult supervision and must be placed in an appropriate container or on a suitable surface away from other flammable materials. They are not to be left unattended.

Put a large label on the box reminding guests that the kit should only be used if the power goes off:

DO NOT OPEN THIS KIT UNLESS THE POWER HAS FAILED

This box contains items for use in the event of a power outage. If items have been removed from the box under any other circumstances, the cost of replacement, together with an administration fee, will be deducted from your damage deposit.

It may seem like we are laboring the point, but experienced owners have stressed the importance of spelling out instructions clearly and succinctly.

"It's to everyone's benefit that nothing is left to chance, so covering all eventualities in the guest guide is the best idea. We put a friendly introduction to a section that we title 'Rules of the House' and list all the important things our renters must be aware of. It seems there are a lot of rules to follow, but we want our guests to have a great time and not be surprised by any of our cottage's eccentricities that we are familiar with."

7
BOOKING SYSTEMS

If you have decided to manage your own rentals rather than use an agency, you will need a comprehensive system for handling bookings. This doesn't have to be complicated but it will have to be consistent, particularly if there is more than one person in your household who will take prospective client calls or handle email inquiries. Good organization is important to prevent overbooking, which unfortunately happens all too often. People will make tentative bookings, change their minds, confirm dates on one day, then cancel the next. You also need to ensure that everyone in the family is aware of your proposed systems.

If you decide to do your own rental management, you will need systems in place to monitor availability, track payments, collect feedback, and evaluate how well your marketing is doing. A simple spreadsheet can take care of this and, providing it is updated regularly to reflect the booking process, can save you precious time and money. It is really worth taking time to do this properly. There is a guest tracking sheet template on the CD.

"We had a situation where my wife was dealing with one request for a two-week rental in the summer over the phone and I was emailing another potential guest with information on the same week. It then became a bit fraught when we both confirmed the weeks with our respective clients and then had to let one party down. We've tightened our system up since then and if I make a phone booking, I just update the availability list that is kept by the phones and then ensure it is transferred immediately to the master availability list on the computer."

Your systems should cover the following:

- Handling inquiries by phone/email
- Creating and managing a database of inquirers
- Reservations
- Updating availability
- Collecting payments and security deposits
- Cancellations
- Information dispatch
- Key handling
- Collecting feedback

From November onwards (and often a lot earlier) your telephone and email will be busy with prospective renters checking availability, asking questions, and hopefully confirming bookings. As exciting as this seems at first, many queries won't end up as bookings as people will be contacting dozens of property owners and rental agencies to select just the right vacation home for them.

"I started out by sending lengthy emails to people, describing the cottage and the surrounding area, and fully expecting them to come back by return to book! I was so disappointed when most didn't even respond to my email. By the time I had the summer booked, I realized that most of the inquiries were so generalized and they were being sent to lots of other owners. I developed a set of standard responses that I could just cut and paste, dependent on the nature of the original request."

FREQUENTLY ASKED QUESTIONS

People ask plenty of questions so it really is worthwhile compiling a list of frequently asked questions. Add this to your website if you have one, and keep the list by the computer or phone so anyone who picks up the request has the answers handy. You can create a standard list that you send to people inquiring by email, which will save time when you are receiving several requests for information each day. Example questions asked most often include:

- Is the waterfront safe for small children/swimming/diving?

- Is access to the dock suitable for elderly people?

- Can we launch our boat from the property or is there a marina nearby?

- What is the fishing like?

- Do you allow pets?

- How far is the nearest general store?

- How are the bedrooms configured? How many twin, double, queen beds, or bunks?

- What is included in the rental (e.g., propane, watercraft, linens?)

- Is the water drinkable?

And the odd ones too!

- It says your cottage sleeps six. We have six adults and eight kids: would that be OK?

- Can we host a wedding at the property? Just a hundred or so day guests, but only four staying the night!

- You say in your ad that you don't take pets. Can my son bring his snake?

HOLDING PERIOD

People will often ask if you can hold the rental period they are looking for while they make up their minds if they want it or not. If you are happy to do this, decide how long this holding period will be and be very firm about it. Usually 24 hours is long enough considering you may be receiving other inquiries during this time. It is not uncommon for people to place a hold on a number of properties so they have all their options covered, and then cherry-pick the best one. You may lose other, better prospects if you give too much leeway. If you have a standard response that clearly states holding times, you won't leave people in any doubt as to where they stand. Even when they have come back to you and said they would like to book, it is still important to let them know that the booking is not final until you have received payment. A short section that can go into an email message states something like this:

> **This is not a confirmed booking until we have received your deposit and completed booking form, although we do allow 3 working days for your payment to reach us.**

Some people will ask to come up and see your property before they confirm and you will need to decide your policy on this. Providing they can visit within the holding period, this should be welcomed as it gives you a chance to meet them, answer any questions they may have, and do a spot of mutual checking as well. If you are going to hold a rental period until a visit happens, make it clear that you will expect a deposit there and then if they decide to go ahead. This is quite fair if you have held off other potential renters in the meantime.

"We had some people who wanted to take a look at the property before they confirmed. That was fine and we arranged for them to come up on the weekend. We had other people who wanted the same week, but we told them we couldn't confirm until these people had visited. They arrived an hour late on the Saturday morning, went through the cottage carrying a checklist, ticking or crossing items off — I think they were scoring each one — then told us they had eight other places to look at before they made their decision the next week. After they left, we emailed the other family and offered the week to them! We couldn't believe it when the people who had visited called several days later to say they had decided to take our home for the week. They were quite put out when we said we had already rented it."

You will also want to ask your potential guests some questions to satisfy yourself they meet your criteria. If you decide not to accept single sex groups (stag and stagettes, for example), groups of young people, or children under a certain age, you will need to collect information on the party before accepting a booking. If you don't make this clear from the start, it may create difficulties if they send their deposit and you have essentially confirmed the booking by the time you discover the make-up of the party doesn't meet your criteria.

RENTAL PERIODS

If you have different rental rates throughout the year, make it clear when your low, mid and high seasons begin and end, and make sure everyone in your family who responds to a booking request knows your policy on weekly versus weekend rental in the summer. It could be quite annoying when you come back from a few days away to find Aunt Marge has rented a weekend in the height of the season for you, when you could easily have rented a full week either side of that weekend.

Your high season may include July, August, Christmas, New Year's, and the Spring break, with higher weekend rates for the long weekends and Valentine's.

It's not unusual to limit your rental period to two-week blocks in the summer if you know from previous experience you will rent in this way with no difficulty. This is quite an economical way of handling summer rentals as the number of turnarounds is halved, and consequently the costs associated with them are reduced substantially.

BOOKING FORM AND RENTAL AGREEMENT

You will need a well-structured booking form, together with a list of the terms and conditions of rental. There are quite a few areas that need to be covered in the rental agreement. As this is a legal document, it must be signed and dated by both parties as acceptance of the rental for the period indicated. There is a sample vacation rental agreement on the CD-ROM that you can adapt to suit your own requirements. Sample 6 is a very basic agreement that covers most points.

The lead party member signs the form on behalf of those listed, so it's important that any guests added after the original booking are included on a supplementary form that can be signed at the start of the rental.

You can prepare your own rental agreement, but have the wording checked with your attorney or lawyer. Some additional points that you may wish to include are:

- Cancellation policy

- Request for references

- Any disclaimers

Party members

If you choose to place restrictions on groups you will rent to, you may want to check references with other owners the party has rented from or with employers. This is perfectly acceptable and

VACATION RENTAL AGREEMENT

Vacation Property Rental Agreement

The following agreement binds a contract between the following parties:

"THE RENTER"
Name
Address

Tel No.

and

"THE OWNER"
Name
Address

Tel No.

The property rented in this agreement is known as [*cottage name*] and is located at [*town*], [*state/province*].

Maximum number of occupants:_____

1. Party Members
Please list all members of your party in the table below. All persons listed will be bound by the terms of this agreement.

First name	Last name	Age	Occupation

2. Rental Period
The period of this rental shall be from [*arrival date*] to [*departure date*]. The property will be ready for occupancy at _____ p.m. on [*arrival date*], and must be vacated by _____ a.m. on [*departure date*] (unless otherwise agreed with THE OWNER).

3. Payment and Security

The rent for the period is $_____, payable as follows:

A deposit of _____ percent is payable when the rental agreement is signed. Checks to be made payable to [*your name*] and sent to:

[*your address*]

The final balance of the rental is due on or before _____ [*30 days before the rental commences*].

OR

Full amount of rental is payable by return mail, together with the signed rental agreement. Checks to be made payable to [*your name*] and sent to:

[*your address*]

A damage deposit of $_____ is also required with the final balance. This will be made out in the form of a separate check, which will not be cashed unless THE OWNER has a valid claim to make upon it (any bills for long-distance or international phone calls will be deducted from this check and a copy of the bill will be forwarded to THE RENTER). If no claims are made, the damage deposit check will be voided and returned four weeks after THE RENTER'S departure from the cottage.

4. Utilities

THE OWNER will provide THE RENTER with water, heat, electricity, linens, and a telephone, which can be used for local calls (all long-distance and international calls will be charged to THE RENTER). All utilities are included in the total rental price.

5. Restrictions

Smoking is not permitted inside the cottage.

Pets are not permitted.

6. Damage Deposit

The cost of any unreasonable damage caused by THE RENTER will be deducted from the damage deposit.

THE RENTER will be responsible for any damage caused in excess of the damage deposit and will be invoiced separately.

The damage deposit check will be voided and returned to THE RENTER by THE OWNER after the cottage owner/caretaker has inspected the property and the phone bill has been cleared.

7. General Conditions

The maximum number of guests using the rental premises shall not exceed the total number stated in the rental agreement.

THE RENTER shall, at his or her expense, and throughout the period of the rental, keep the property in a state of cleanliness and in good condition and repair. THE RENTER acknowledges that at commencement of the rental the property is in good and substantial repair except for any defect THE RENTER may report to THE OWNER'S representative during the first day of the rental. THE RENTER shall leave the property in good repair, cleaned, and vacuumed, and shall leave the dishes washed, beds stripped, and all garbage separated appropriately in sealed garbage bags and placed tidily in the garage. The cleaning checklist shall be completed and signed.

Any unsafe or dangerous conditions must be reported to THE OWNER'S representative immediately. THE RENTER acknowledges that the use of the property is entirely at THE RENTER'S risk. THE RENTER shall indemnify and save harmless THE OWNER against and from any and all expenses, costs, damages, suits, actions, or liabilities arising from any and all loss of or damage to personal property, injury, or death resulting from the use of the rental property, grounds, boats, bicycles, and river/lake use.

THE RENTER assumes full responsibility for fulfilling the terms of the rental for the period stated.

Signatures:

Owner:_____   Date:_____

Renter:_____   Date:_____

most renters won't mind being asked to provide references. I suggest you include reference checks on your booking form. If it seems clear the party has rented before — you can ask this at the outset — but your contact is reluctant to provide details of the previous rental, regard this with suspicion. Your peace of mind comes with creating a good relationship with those renting your property, so it's important that you are comfortable with them. You may find after talking with them on the phone, or several email messages, that you are happy with their credentials and don't feel the need to check references. This is your decision; after a few bookings you'll settle on a policy for this.

Decide on the maximum number of people that can use the property and be clear about this. If it is a large home, you will attract larger parties so you might want to restrict this to family groups rather than, say, several couples. Or you may prefer couples over families.

"We've been renting our cottage for four years now and the only problem we ever had was with a group of two families, each with a nanny. They were extremely demanding, calling us almost every day with requests for this and that. They left a real mess when they departed and we ended up claiming the full damage deposit to pay for breakages and cleaning expenses. We've rented to parties of six couples before, and when they have left, we would not have known they had been there, the place was so clean and tidy."

Only you can decide how far you want to go in the vetting process. One couple who own several properties feel they make good judgments by talking to prospective renters on the phone. They have developed questions to establish how reliable renters will be. Many rental agencies require other evidence, such as insurance documents or a driver's license, to show date of birth, occupation, etc. What it boils down to is that there is risk in this business as in any other; it is just that the risk here is an emotional one as well as a practical one. Therefore, you need to balance your emotional attachment to your home with your desire to maximize the investment you have made. If you leave valuable ornaments and antiques out, there is a risk they will get broken. If you have a handmade oak dining table, there is a risk it may be scratched or stained with candle wax; if you leave your cedar canoe for your guests to use, there is a risk it will be damaged. However much you exhort your guests to look after your things, they will not have the same emotional attachment to them as you have. This is not to say they will not respect your personal and valued items, just that there is a risk.

RENTAL PERIOD: DATES AND TIMES

You must be very specific about when your cottage will be available for occupancy by your guests and by what time they must vacate: an error or misunderstanding could cause embarrassment, not to mention inconvenience to all concerned. For example, your rental agreement could state:

> The period of rental begins at 4 p.m. on Saturday, July 26th and ends at 11 a.m. on Saturday, August 2nd, unless otherwise agreed with THE OWNER.

If you have back-to-back rentals, don't forget to allow sufficient time for the turnaround. Allowing three to four hours should be about right, although if you are using a property management company they will probably appreciate a longer gap if they are covering several changeovers on a Saturday or Sunday.

PAYMENTS AND DEPOSITS

People will expect to pay a deposit to secure their rental. How much you decide to charge "up front" is up to you. Approximately 25 percent to 35 percent is the norm. Make it clear that the deposit must be received within a specified number of days from taking the booking. One owner uses this wording:

> If the nonrefundable minimum deposit is not received within three working days of THE OWNER-confirmed booking, the booking will be considered canceled. THE OWNER then has the right to assign the property to another renter for the same rental period.

If you take a late booking and there is no time for payment to arrive by mail, ask your guests to bring a money order or certified check, along with their security deposit.

CANCELLATIONS

Consider how you will deal with cancellations and make your cancellation policy clear and unequivocal. You may decide to accept cancellations if you are able to rebook the period that has been cancelled. However, charging an administration fee is also quite acceptable and may deter those people who will book a vacation home early in the season to at least secure a rental, and then cancel later if they find something that appears more appealing. You may use a graduated scale of cancellation charges that increases the later the cancellation occurs. State your cancellation policy in the rental agreement. For overseas visitors, their travel insurance should cover cancellation in the event of illness, accident, or death of a close relative or person traveling in the party prior to the rental. With this in mind, it is worthwhile encouraging all your guests to take out sufficient travel insurance to cover them in a range of situations.

A fair cancellation policy would include a full refund of all payments if the cancellation is made before four weeks of the vacation commencing, providing the rental period is able to be rented to another party. After that time you could adopt a sliding scale of refund dependent on the weeks remaining before the rental start date. So, if the vacation is cancelled the week before, you could offer a refund of 75 percent if you were able to rent the complete period to another party. You have then retained 25 percent that will cover the additional costs you have incurred in marketing and advertising that period of time. Your wording could be as follows:

Cancellation Policy

In the event you have to cancel your booking at the Lake House and we are able to rebook the full amount or a portion of the rental period, refund of your payment will be made as follows:

- More than 45 days before the vacation commences: full amount of deposit

- Less than 45 days but more than 30 days before the vacation commences: 90 percent of payment made

- Fewer than 30 days but more than 14 days before the vacation commences: 80 percent of payment made

- Fewer than 14 days before the vacation commences: 75 percent of payment made

You will find that having a solid cancellation policy will deter people from including your property in their multiple bookings and will save you from trying to find alternative renters at the last minute.

DAMAGE/SECURITY DEPOSIT

Holding a damage/security deposit is your insurance against damage that may occur beyond normal wear and tear and minor breakages that you should allow for. For example, a broken glass or two, a minor wine stain on a carpet, or a tear in a sheet or towel could be considered normal wear and tear. A burn in a carpet, significant candle wax splashes, missing items, or substantial breakage would be grounds for claims on the damage deposit. Amounts between $400 and $1,000 are commonly charged as damage deposits, and will depend on the size of the property, the number of people it sleeps, and the value of furnishings. It is not customary for a damage deposit check to be cashed prior to occupancy, although it's not unknown.

It is always worth adding an additional clause in the rental agreement stating that any damage caused by negligence amounting to more than the damage deposit will be invoiced separately and must be paid promptly. Make sure your renters understand that you need to know if things get broken so that you can replace them before the next rental. Often, they may neglect to mention minor damage or breakages because they worry about being charged, so be up front on the issue at the outset and your renters will be more comfortable with letting you know if they have had an accident of any kind. For example, a carpet stain will be more easily removed if treated quickly than if it is left to the end of the rental. Wilful damage is, of course, another issue and one that should be covered by a good insurance policy. Talk with your insurance broker about this so you are in no doubt about having sufficient coverage.

State what you do with the damage deposit following the end of the rental period. If your phone is not blocked for long-distance calls, you will need to check the phone bill before returning the deposit check. Alternatively, if you are happy with the condition of the property, return the deposit promptly along with a feedback questionnaire. If you have a claim on the deposit, let your renters know promptly exactly what you are charging them for and why. You can then cash the check, retain the amount required to rectify the damage, and send them the balance.

"I take my digital camera when I go to check the cottage and if there is an issue involving the damage deposit, I take a couple of photos. Then we have proof of damage. It hasn't happened often since we have been renting, but when we have had a claim, the photos were helpful in explaining why we were charging the renters."

ADDITIONAL CLAUSES

Make clear your policy on pets, smoking, additional guests — both day and overnight visitors — and what you expect your guests to do prior to checkout. Policies on cleaning differ depending on the general standard for your area. In Ontario cottage country, for example, most owners will expect their guests to leave the property cleaned and readied for the next guests. This is because many of these properties are in remote locations that would prevent a property management company from reaching more than one or possibly two during the changeover period. So, although the cottages are checked at a changeover period, full cleaning may not be possible at an affordable rate.

If you are including watercraft with your vacation rental, particularly motorized vessels, you'll need a specific disclaimer, which should be checked by your lawyer. Otherwise, a general disclaimer is all that you need here. A typical one might read as follows:

Any unsafe or dangerous condition must be reported to the Owner's representative immediately. The Renter acknowledges that the use of the property is entirely at the Renter's risk. The Renter shall indemnify and save harmless the Owner against and from any and all expenses, costs, damages, suits, actions, or liabilities arising from any and all loss of or damage to personal property, injury, or death resulting from the use of the rental property, grounds, boats, bicycles, and river/lake use.

8
SEASONAL RENTALS

For recreational properties located in winter hot spots, there is a great opportunity to offer seasonal rental. This has lots of advantages, but there are also some drawbacks that you should consider before you start promoting your property in this market. Make sure you know what you want out of the rental or you may find yourself in the following situation:

"We rented our vacation home to a group of four people wanting to snowmobile on weekends. Because they only wanted weekends, we decided not to offer it on a seasonal rental basis and billed them at a weekend rate. We were then able to open it up to midweek rentals. What then happened was a real learning experience. Every Monday we went up there to do the changeover after the weekend, including laundry, cleaning, etc., but we only got one or two additional midweek rentals in the entire season. In retrospect, it would have been much more cost-effective to charge our weekend snowmobilers for the full season, which would have saved us the time and effort we spent on the changeovers. The gross income may have been marginally less, but we could have passed on heating, lighting, and fuel expenses, which we ultimately ended up paying."

THE MARKET FOR SEASONAL RENTALS

Many people buy properties for investment in well-known ski areas with the primary aim of offering winter rentals and reaping the rewards of this lucrative market. If it is a condo or chalet in a resort development, you may be bound by a restrictive covenant on the deed or management contract, so check this out to start with. If not, check your competitors to find out what they are charging and follow their lead. In these developments, unless you have a unique selling point such as being situated in a ski-in/ski-out location or a high-demand area, staying in line with other rental units should offer the best return on your marketing investment.

If your vacation home is in a warm winter location you will benefit from the "snowbird" market, as Canadians and northern US folks exchange life in the freezer for a more moderate climate. Florida, Arizona, and California are popular destinations.

RESEARCH THE COMPETITION

Good research is a must to make sure your rental is competitive and matches up with other similar vacation homes in your area. A great way of researching the competition is to call several agencies or owners, and ask for their rates and seasonal package information. In a resort development, this should be fairly straightforward, as additional costs such as heating, snow clearance, and maintenance are likely to be included. If your chalet is individually located you can be more creative in your rental package, but it is still a good idea to find out what the standard seasonal features are. Make a list of what is to be included and what should be charged at an additional fee, then prepare your rental agreement laying all these things out clearly.

HOW TO PRICE YOUR SEASONAL RENTAL

A season means a complete period of time running from three to five months. Your competitive research should give you a ballpark figure for the accommodation you have to offer, and some indication of what is usually included in this figure.

A seasonal rate usually covers a set period of time, and a rental contract clearly states what is included in that price and what is considered an "extra" charge. In general terms, the following features and facilities will need to be covered in a seasonal rental contract:

- *Snow clearance.* This covers access to the property and may or may not include driveways. The contract should be clear on the boundaries of snow clearance and identify the restrictions on vehicle parking.

- *Telephone connection.* A monthly telephone fee is usually included, with long-distance calls billed separately.

- *Satellite TV.* Including a basic package is customary; however, the inclusion of additional programming may be negotiated within the contract.

- *Internet connection.* A basic rate should be included, with any additional hours (if applicable) charged separately.

- *Heating.* This can be a significant expense, and electricity is usually charged as an extra cost, over and above the seasonal rental fee. Where oil and propane are the major source of heating, consider filling the tank at the start of the rental, and topping up at the end. You can then charge the renter an accurate figure for fuel usage.

- *Wood.* Where wood is the primary source of heat, you can provide a supply to last the season and include the cost in the rental fee. Or guests may bring in their own or buy it locally themselves. Or you can offer wood at an additional cost as these owners did:

"With one chalet, we had already purchased two cords of wood which were drying at the back of the house. We decided to offer the cords to our renters for purchase in addition to the rental cost, since they indicated they'd probably use all of it — they accepted and purchased the two cords at an additional charge."

Seasonal properties are generally fully equipped with furniture, linens, dishes, a starter supply of cleaning supplies, and toiletries. Comprehensive instructions should be included in the form of a chalet guide regarding TV/DVD/satellite operation, garbage disposal instructions, local telephone numbers, and emergency instructions.

"This year, for both our properties, we charged a rental fee from November 15th to April 15th (to coincide with the ski season). Since the ski season typically runs for five months, it made sense to have the incoming renters responsible for hydro, and we contacted Quebec Hydro to change the billing to our renters' names for the duration. We took a meter reading on the day of check-in and will take another on checkout. A few weeks prior to checkout we'll inform the power company of the date we will be resuming billing responsibilities."

— *Owner of a vacation rental in Mont Tremblant, Quebec*

SECURITY/DAMAGE DEPOSIT

For short-term vacation rentals a security or damage deposit is taken to cover breakages or damage that go beyond normal wear and tear. A seasonal rental brings with it the potential for higher costs that you will want to recover without argument after the rental period is over. These are costs for heating, telephone, Internet, and any other incidental costs that may arise. To ensure you are not out of pocket, collect a substantial deposit, making it clear within your contract what this will be used for. The deposit can cover your projected costs and be reassessed at the end of the season with the difference refunded.

SCREENING RENTERS

It is important to screen your rental guests for any vacation rental, and particularly so for those who will occupy the property for a longer period of time. Whereas a short-term rental guest will be fully aware of the temporary nature of their stay, a seasonal guest will tend to treat the property more as their own over the longer time. If their standards are significantly lower than yours, this may lead to a mismatch of expectations and issues over damage on the termination of the agreement. Of course, you can never guarantee that the renters you have carefully selected are going to leave the place in the exact state in which it was found, but thorough screening can go a long way to prevent potentially difficult situations from arising. Here's some useful advice from a "seasoned" seasonal owner.

"Our experience so far has been through word of mouth/ referrals, so the people renting have already been validated to a certain extent. I would recommend for cases where the renter is 'unknown' that a rental application be emailed to prospective renters asking for names of people who will be staying with ages of children noted, workplace address/ telephone numbers, and three references that you can call to confirm suitability."

THE CONTRACT

A clear and unambiguous rental agreement or contract is necessary so that both parties to the agreement know their responsibilities, and the owner is protected if any issues arise.

The start date and end date of the rental must be stated, as should the total rental fee and schedule of payments. Think carefully about what should be included. Here are some examples of clauses to include:

- Restriction on subletting

- A statement that the property is to be used for residential purposes only by designated people (noted in agreement)

- Owner to be informed for absences of more than X days

- Guest policy, that is, guests can stay a maximum of X consecutive days — this is to allow for holiday guests, but to ensure others don't stay and use facilities for the duration.

- Only dry firewood may be burned in the fireplace

- The renter has a renters insurance policy (typically included with one's primary residence insurance)

- Any plumbing issues or damage caused by renter is their responsibility to correct

- Full cleaning and linen wash must be completed prior to final departure and the property must be returned in the same condition as at beginning of term

You also need to stipulate who should be contacted in the case of maintenance issues or emergencies — for example, a burst pipe or heating malfunction. Our renters need to contact us first, and then we decide whether we want to visit and check out the issue and possibly do the repairs ourselves. We then make the arrangements to have our preferred company visit or conduct repairs should this be necessary. This ensures repairs are valid and necessary, prior to us incurring costs.

Finally, the agreement should contain witnessed signatures of both parties.

PAYMENT SCHEDULES

Decide on how you want payments to be made. A schedule using postdated checks may be right for you, or you might prefer a substantial deposit and a second payment made midway through the rental period. A suitable deposit could be from 30 percent to 50 percent of the total cost.

The agreement should state that failure to meet a payment would result in premature termination of the rental agreement, at the discretion of the owner.

Overholding

"Overholding" is a term used to describe a situation where a tenant does not vacate at the end of a tenancy, and is most often found in landlord/tenant agreements that come within state or provincial landlord/tenant legislation. As seasonal rentals are generally classed outside such legislation, it is simply necessary to add a clause on the rental agreement that classifies the accommodation as a vacation rental. This acts as a safety net for the owner by reinforcing the nature of the rental.

If you choose to include a clause on overholding in a seasonal rental contract, you are advised to check on the applicable legislation in the state or province where your vacation home is located.

WHAT IS THE DOWNSIDE OF SEASONAL RENTALS?

Renting seasonally has some serious benefits. Apart from the contracted maintenance, snow clearance, etc., while your renters are in residence, you don't have the cost of changeovers. All being well, you'll have a problem-free season and can pocket a substantial rental check that should take care of all your expenses, with a good amount left over. However, before you commit, do your homework carefully; make your agreement watertight; have it checked by a legal advisor; and above all, be happy with your decision to rent for the season. If you regret not being able to use the property yourself, or worry for the whole time that it is being misused, this is not the route for you!

9
MARKETING YOUR VACATION HOME

You may have decided to appoint a rental agency to handle all your bookings and be content with the renters they find for you, accepting that this method will eat a substantial proportion of your rental income in commission payments. With the right agency, you should feel fully confident that you'll have rental income for at least eight weeks of the year — certainly the high-season weeks and perhaps some long weekends — Christmas and New Year's, Thanksgiving, and other public holidays. However, it is worth bearing in mind that your agency probably represents dozens, and sometimes hundreds, of other properties, each of which has owners who are as keen as you are to rent as many weeks as possible. Chapter 10 suggests ways of working proactively with your agent to see what additional methods there are of promoting your recreational home. This chapter is for those of you who plan to do your own marketing and are prepared to commit to the time needed to plan a campaign and actively carry it out.

WHAT IS MARKETING?

Marketing is a big subject! Whole degree courses are devoted to it, and bookstores offer thick books on the theory and practice. For the purposes of this book it is sufficient to consider the basic principles and how they relate to vacation rental.

Key in "what is marketing?" on Google and one definition you will find is:

> The process of planning and executing the conception, pricing, promotion, and distribution of goods, services, and ideas to create exchanges that satisfy individual and organization objectives.

Ouch! Doesn't that sound like the foreword to an introductory marketing course? On searching a little further, the next two quotations seem to sum up what marketing is all about in much clearer language:

> Marketing is the art of making someone want something you have.

> Marketing deals with two important things: money and emotions.

These definitions are a lot easier to understand and offer a much better picture of what marketing is, so let's stick with them for the time being.

First, it is useful to understand the differences between all those things we commonly talk about under the general title of marketing. This quote from an unknown source describes it very well:

> "If the circus is coming to town and you paint a sign saying 'Circus Coming to the Fairground Saturday,' that's *advertising*. If you put the sign on the back of an elephant and walk it into town, that's *promotion*. If the elephant walks through the mayor's flower bed, that's *publicity*. And if you get the mayor to laugh about it, that's *public relations*. If the town's citizens go to the circus, you show them the

many entertainment booths, explain how much fun they'll have spending money at the booths, answer their questions and ultimately, they spend a lot at the circus, that's *sales*."

With this in mind, it's not enough to post a sign at the end of your driveway saying "House to Rent," and stick an ad on the bulletin board in the local grocery store. To sell rental weeks in your property, you will need to think about different methods of marketing it, such as advertising, developing your own website and promoting it, and alternative ways of getting people to see your property as the place where they want to spend their hard-earned vacation money. This requires a fair amount of planning and research. It's not sufficient to sign up to a free web advertising offer and sit back and wait for bookings to pour in — this won't happen. Your marketing plan will help you develop the most effective and economical strategy to reach the people you want to buy from you.

Companies will typically spend between 10 percent and 15 percent of their projected turnover on advertising and promotion. For a vacation home rental business, this level of investment is not necessary; however, it is good practice to decide what profit you want to yield and plan your strategy accordingly. Of course, your outlay during the first year of rental will probably be higher than in future years because you need to experiment to find out what works for you, commission a website, and get yourself established as a serious rental business.

"Our outlay for the first time we rented was quite high as we went to a web design company to do our site, and we tried out a few advertisements with online agencies. Almost immediately, we got lots of emails and telephone calls which showed our advertising had worked. What we forgot to do from the start was ask every person who inquired where they had found us. That would have given us a better idea on which ad was working the best!"

The marketing plan is the framework for your rental business. It will ensure you do adequate research, consider a range of different marketing options, and limit your expenditure to those opportunities that are really going to make it work for you. Don't forget that your marketing plan starts with having your goals clearly stated, because when you know how much profit you want to make, you'll be in a better position to make good decisions on how to market your cottage.

THE POWER OF THE INTERNET

Our experience shows that over 90 percent of inquiries for our rental properties are generated from an Internet search — and this is probably a conservative estimate. To succeed in renting a vacation home, you will need to have a web presence — either by using one or more of the vacation rental advertising sites to market your property, or by setting up and promoting your own website. In fact if you have a website, you will be placing links to it from many other websites to maximize your exposure. It could be argued that there is little need to set up your own site as there are so many advertising sites keen to attract your listing; however, developing your own unique web presence may well be worth it in the long run. Let's look at this option first.

YOUR OWN WEBSITE

Having your own website can prove invaluable to your vacation home. Once on the web, your site becomes an inexpensive advertising tool as, apart from the cost of initial design, then ongoing hosting and updating expense, there is little that needs to be spent on it. You are able to advertise widely on other sites with a link to your own. And if you are familiar with some of the web design software and have some graphic design capabilities, even getting started won't be too much a burden on the budget. Getting your site well ranked on the search engines costs nothing but your time and effort, and you'll reap benefits in terms of the bookings generated. However, if the site is poorly developed and no one can find it, the time and money invested will be wasted. There are plenty of bad websites out there that demonstrate this.

Start your research by looking at other vacation rental sites. Put yourself in the shoes of a potential rental guest and go searching for a property in your area. Key in the words you would use to find a place — for example, *vacation home New England*; *villa Sedona Arizona*; *waterfront cottage Ontario*. First to come up will most likely be the rental advertising sites and that is useful too, so add those addresses to your favorites list. Take a look at the top listed sites and pick out a few properties that catch your interest. If they have links to individual rental property sites, click on several and pay critical attention to how each site is presented. List what you like and what you don't, paying particular attention to design, ease of navigation, and general user-friendliness.

This marks the start of your web market research, and it is important that you don't just surf around without keeping a log of your findings. If you use an Excel spreadsheet for tracking your research, you'll find when you type in the web address it will be hyperlinked so you can get back to it easily. Make a note of the key words you used to find the sites as these will be helpful in your own site development.

Headings for your spreadsheet can include the following:

- Web address

- Key words used

- Advertising site it was listed on

- Presentation

- Usability

- What you liked most

- What you liked least

Of course you can use as many headings as you want as long as the information you are gathering will come in useful when planning your site. You could also look on the site for information on the web designer. Sometimes this is included at the foot of the page with a link to the designer's site, which can be helpful when comparing web design costs.

Your web address

The whole idea of having your own website is for it to be found by people looking for a recreational property to rent. There is no point in having a good-looking site if no one can find it, which can easily happen if you opt for the cheapest hosting option. This is usually a personal web page offered at no cost by an Internet service provider.

Most Internet service providers (ISPs) allow their users to set up personal web pages as part of a basic Internet account. This looks attractively inexpensive; however, this method of marketing your site has drawbacks. First, your URL (the web address assigned to your site) will look something like this:

http://yourserviceprovider/yourdomain/

The problem with this is that some search engines such as Yahoo! won't list your site if it is clearly an ISP site. Second, if you change your ISP for any reason, you will have to change your web address (URL). People who have visited your site before will not be able to find it again, and any advertising you have listing the URL will have to be changed.

It looks much more professional if you register your own domain name rather than opt for your ISP's personal page site. Your site would then be www.yourdomain.com or www.yourdomain.ca. You'll have to pay for this service, but you will have more opportunity to expand your site, if, for example, you buy a second rental property.

The alternative to using your ISP's free space is to find a web host that will host your site on their server for a monthly fee. Besides being able to use your unique URL, they will register it for you, allow you a certain amount of space for your website and a number of email addresses, depending on the package you buy. This means you can have unique email addresses for different purposes such as yourname@yourdomain.ca or inquiries@yourdomain.ca.

When search engines rate a site they often look at the web address first. Say you are in northern California. An address containing the words *vacation*, *rental*, *Sonoma*, *Napa*, or a combination of them will increase your chance of improving your rating. If you think about your own Internet surfing behavior, you probably don't go beyond the first three or so pages found on a search. Research shows that most people don't, so the trick is to make sure your site appears in those first three pages. Whatever you can do to get your site up there will pay dividends in the future. Do bear in mind, though, that it can take weeks or even months for the search engines to find your site and index it in their directories!

Choosing the name for your website is fun but it can also be frustrating when you find that the great name that suddenly came to you in the middle of the night has already been taken. However, finalizing a name is the first thing you should do once you have decided to have a website to promote your business.

If you haven't already thought of a name for your site, brainstorm with family or colleagues. Here are a few pointers:

- Make sure your web name reflects your property and is descriptive, such as *lakeshorehome* or *redrockretreat* or *sunsethideaway*. Be realistic, though. Naming your property after something far more grandiose than it actually is can backfire. For example, if you have a log cabin in the woods, it is probably not a good idea to have the word *chateau* in the web name, although *chalet* might be OK. Similarly, although you might consider your vacation paradise to be a *mansion* in a tongue-in-cheek way, it is not a good idea to use this in a descriptive title or you may find yourself accused of misrepresentation!

- Keep the name as short as you can. Although you do have up to 67 characters, a longer name can bring problems, not least of which is the difficulty people may have in remembering it. And it can be potentially frustrating every time you have to repeat the name over the phone.

- Avoid using hyphens or underscoring as this again can cause confusion.

- The .com extension is one most people recognize, and if you can get that one, it's great. If not, try your country extension, such as .us or .ca. Formerly obscure extensions such as .net and .org are becoming more common too.

Go to one of the domain name search websites, such as www.cheekydomains.com, and type in the name you have chosen along with the extensions you want (.com, .us, .ca, etc). This will tell you if the name is available. You can either register it yourself for a small fee, or, if you have chosen a web hosting company, they may offer free domain registration as part of a web hosting package. If you have found a web design company you want to work with, they may also offer to do the registration for you. If they do, make sure the domain will be registered in your name and that there will not be an additional cost. It is not unknown for a low-cost web design company to offer to register for you, then put the domain in their name. Then, when you want to update the site, they can charge as much as they want, as you are then unable to change to another company without losing your domain name. A lot of online companies offer web design at discount prices. If you are tempted by these offers take a careful look at what you get for your money — it is often a very limited deal.

Working with a web designer

The cost of developing a website will mainly depend on how many pages you have on your site, although individual web design companies may set prices in different ways. In general, expect to pay anywhere between $800 and $1,200 for a professionally designed website. The costs of maintaining an active website vary markedly, starting as low as $5 per month. With today's technology there is no particular advantage to using a local web hosting company. Do your research online and you may find the best prices are a long way from home.

If you decide to engage a web designer, you may find someone local to your property who does this type of work. Creating a good relationship with someone you can sit down with and explain the look you want can result in a classy site that does what you want it to do. Small website builders are able to offer this personal service relatively inexpensively, and because they have local knowledge they are more likely to understand your needs. Take a look at the other sites they have designed, talk to their clients, and ask questions about cost, how long it will take, and how maintenance and updating will be carried out. A good site will need regular updating, so you need to know how much that will cost. Ask for a statistics program to be included so that you can monitor the traffic visiting your website.

The relationship you have with your web designer is important, as you will have ideas that you want translated into creative design for your site and the designer may have his or her own ideas that conflict with yours. Take the time to find someone you can work with comfortably — this will pay dividends in the future. Keep in mind that redoing a website can be just as expensive as the initial design work, so changing your mind after the event could be prohibitive financially.

Bear in mind that the web designer's job is to create an attractive site that is structured in such a way that it is easy to navigate and will encourage visitors to stay on the site. Your job is to provide the text and the photographs and present clear direction to the designer about the look and feel you want for your website. The designer will want to know what you want your site to achieve; the type of site traffic you are looking for; how many pages you want; what additional functions you'd like, such as a calendar or the ability for your potential renters to fill out forms online.

Some small web designers may be happy to teach you simple aspects of the software package they have used to develop your site in order for you to make minor changes, which will save you money.

There is a world of difference between a professionally designed and developed site and one that is clearly homemade, so unless you have the skill to develop a fully functional and attractive site, this may be a task best left to a web designer. A good web designer has both the technical skills to put together a clear and easily navigable site, and the graphic design capability needed to make it visually attractive and compelling. If you have the time and expertise, you can of course build your own site, and there is plenty of help available online. Searching on "building websites," "low cost web design," or similar phrases should provide you with just about everything you need to know to do it yourself, from registering a domain name through designing and creating effective websites, to finding a host and, most important of all, how to get people to look at your site.

It is easy to fall into the trap of thinking the do-it-yourself option is a cheap and easy one; however, it can be very costly if you don't have the technical and design skills that are required.

Site content

You want people to visit your website and stay there, rather than clicking away somewhere else too quickly. The way to do this is to make your site "sticky" (a term for a site that has enough interest to make visitors stick around). Clean and clear sites do this for most people; cluttered, messy sites with patterned backgrounds do not! Your home page should not only be readable and attractive, it should show your visitors in the first three seconds what your site is about.

Assuming you are using a web designer to develop the graphic and technical part of the site, your task is to think about the three main aspects of a great website:

- Structure
- Text
- Images

Site structure

The structure and layout of a site is important so your visitors can find their way around with ease. A simple site may have only a few pages that are linked from the home page. One page might be on the property itself; one on attractions and events in the area; one your booking terms and conditions and your rates. You may also want a "Links" page, particularly if you are offering to exchange links with other sites that are related to yours.

A more complicated site may include a calendar — which is always a good idea. The calender offered by www.rentors.org is used by many vacation renters. You can include forms on your website for guests to make inquiries about your property, make reservations, and provide feedback on their experience. Rentors.org also offers an online guest book option, as well as the opportunity to collect payment by credit card. Just make sure you know what options you want before you start with the website design, as incorporating them later can be costly.

Draw a simple flowchart to simplify the task of communicating your needs to your designer. The following is an idea of a web design flowchart that shows how each page links to the next one.

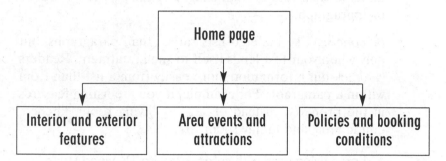

Writing for your website

Web users are busy people: they want to get straight to the facts. They typically don't read a page from start to finish on the computer screen. Instead, they scan a site looking for relevant items, picking out individual words and sentences, and then print pages that contain the information they want. With this in mind, you need to apply a style and method to your web text that accommodates this type of reading. You can guide the reader by highlighting the salient points in the text using headings, lists, and typographical emphasis — using bold and shading to make a point.

- *Summarize first.* Put the main points in the first paragraph so that readers scanning your pages will not miss your point. At the same time, include your key words in this summary as this may help your site get higher rankings with search engines. For example, if your property is in Lake Tahoe you might want to include key words such as *skiing, water sports, North Star, Incline,* and *vacation rental*:

> Beautiful Lake Tahoe vacation rental home. Ski at North Star; canoe the Truckee River; explore the lakefront and visit Tahoe Village and Incline. Our lovely four-bedroom home sleeps eight people comfortably and overlooks the golf course at North Star. An all-season base for every activity or for just plain relaxing!

- *Use one idea per paragraph.* Users will skip over any additional ideas if they are not caught by the first few words in the paragraph.

- *Be concise.* Use bulleted lists rather than paragraphs, but only when your text lends itself to such treatment. Readers can pick out information more easily from a list than from within a paragraph. For example, if you are listing features in the property, instead of saying, "living room, kitchen, dining area, and family room," try this:

  - Large living area with sofas, satellite TV, wood stove, and stereo

  - Dining area with seating for eight

  - Well-stocked fitted kitchen with dishwasher, microwave, and a range of small appliances

  - Great family room with lots of seating and a variety of toys, games, and books

- *Use meaningful subheadings rather than "clever" ones.* For example: "What to see and do in the area," rather than "Mountain Magic."

- *Keep the word count to approximately half of what you would use in conventional writing.* Reading from computer screens is about 25 percent slower than reading on paper, and reading online text is tiring. As a result, people don't want to read a lot of text from computer screens: you should write 50 percent less text rather than just 25 percent less since it's not only a matter of reading speed but also a matter of feeling good.

- *Keep your pages short.* In general, readers don't like to scroll down a page.

- *Include a links page that lists places of interest and other local information sites.* For example, marinas, tourist offices, hiking and biking trails, restaurants, etc. This makes your site more "sticky" and helps with link popularity.

Photographs

Good photographs are critical for enticing interest in your property. People will believe what they see in a photo over and above any text that accompanies it, so using plenty of attractive pictures in your advertising material is important in attracting potential customers.

Exterior photos

Pick a bright, clear day for taking your exterior shots and do your preparation before you start shooting the photos. Take someone unfamiliar with the property with you as they are more likely to notice aspects of the place that you would not. Do a critical walkabout first, looking at the exterior of the property from all angles. Which view is most attractive? Although you want to take great photos, your goal should not be to hide anything either. It is fine to add things to make your place look more attractive but if you are doing this, make sure they are still there for your guests to enjoy (seasons permitting!).

If you are buying a property in the spring and only have photos of your dream home surrounded by melting snow with muddy patches, you could ask the sellers if they have summer photos you can borrow and scan.

Clear the area around the rental property and make sure the picture you take does not include clutter — pool toys, towels, ashtrays, etc. This might seem obvious, but a look at some vacation rental sites demonstrates all too clearly a lack of attention to detail that seriously detracts from the impression the owner is trying to give.

A photo of a hot tub looks much better if the cover is off and the jets are on; watercraft should be on the water and not just upside down on the bank; arrange chairs around a patio table and put up the umbrella — then add a vase of flowers. One owner suggested:

"Select photos that convey the image you want, rather than just showing the items you want people to see. For example, a lake photo may appear black or grey if taken on a cloudy day. A shot taken from the same location on a sunny day, however, reveals a deep blue reflection of an azure summer sky, the subtle shades of green of the lakeside pine forest, and deep reds of sand. The items in both photos may be identical, but the latter conveys what the vacation experience is all about."

— *Craig White, www.cottagelink.com*

Interior photos

Pay even more attention to interior shots. With a digital camera you can experiment with different lighting at different times of day. Remove all clutter from kitchen and lounges and make up the beds with attractive linens. So many websites show dull, functional bedroom photos when it would only take a few minutes to create an eye-catching image. Here are a few more ideas:

- Set the dining table with table linens, a vase of flowers, wine glasses, and matching dinnerware.

- If you plan on renting in the winter season and have a wood-burning stove or open fireplace, have a photo with the fire lit.

- Use appropriate decorative accents to promote seasonal and festive rentals.

- If the kitchen looks bare and functional, brighten it up with colored storage jars; silk flower accents on upper cupboard casings; baskets of fruit and vegetables, etc.

- Brighten white bathrooms with matching colored towels and washcloths.

- Decorate blank walls in bedrooms with inexpensive pictures or framed landscape photos.

If you need more ideas on how to dress up the property for photos, just get a couple of kitchen, bath, and bedroom magazines and check out the staged photos in there. They'll inspire you!

"We chose our rental property because the inside pictures made it look so romantic. There were candles lit and the open fire was going. We knew the lake was across a road, but after seeing the photo of the lake view from the bedroom window, we were sold. If there had just been a description of it without such great pictures, we might not have gone for it — and would have missed a lovely cottage."

Testimonials

The most effective and cheapest form of advertising is by word of mouth. If you leave a guest book in your cottage, write a note at the front of it asking for recommendations on places to visit and things to do. You'll find that your guests often write great messages at the end of their vacation and you can then ask for their permission to use them in your marketing literature and on your website. If you also send guests a post-vacation questionnaire, ask them to write a short testimonial saying what they enjoyed most about their holiday. Perhaps even ask them to send you digital photographs that you can upload onto your website. If you decide to have a special page for these, give it a suitable title that is easy to recognize, for example, "What our guests say."

You can download a free online guest book from www.rentors.org. Ask you web designer to add this to your site, in a format that your guests can use easily. Naturally you will only want to use positive comments — hopefully that is all you will get, but occasionally even the weather can cause guests to be negative about their experience, so monitor this part of your site regularly.

Getting your site seen

Creating an effective linking strategy should be an important part of any online marketing plan. The more people you can get to visit your website, the more inquiries you will get, so work will be necessary on linking your site to others and getting others to link to you.

Link your website to other specialist sites. If your property is on waterfront or near a great lake for fishing, you can list it for free on fishing-related sites (search for "fishing holidays" for examples). Look for addresses of clubs and societies where you can advertise without charge. Other sites will often want to know how you can help them, which you can do if the content of their site is relevant to yours — for example, canoe clubs, snowmobile associations, etc. Offering links to local tourist attractions and places of interest will add interest to your site while increasing your visibility elsewhere.

Look on the web for sites that will let you have a free listing. The site www.alexa.com will let you check on your competitors and see who links to them. You can then look at these links and see if they offer opportunities to list with them. This can all be a time-consuming business but will be well worthwhile in the long run, as the more links you have coming into your site, the more likely people will visit it. Your local chamber of commerce and tourism office are also good sites to link to.

Beware of adding pop-ups or banner advertising on your site. Not only do they clutter it up, reducing the impact of your rental property, they are also intensely annoying to most people. Many viewers may leave your site, never to return.

Search engines and directories

Search engines

Search engines use computer programs called *robots* or *spiders* to automatically go from page to page through the web, reading content and adding it to their databases. Some index words in the title, URL, introductory paragraphs, or full text of all documents on a website. Some use a combination of these words and phrases, all of which are entered into the search engine's database. To speed up the process of getting your site indexed, they usually have a way for you to submit your site for indexing. You usually only have to tell a search engine the URL (address) of your site, and it takes care of the rest. Google and Alta Vista are examples of search engines.

Directories

Directories are run by people who review websites and categorize them within their directories. This leads to a more abridged set of sites, which can be good or bad depending on what you're searching for. Yahoo! and The Open Directory Project are the two biggest directories on the web, but other important directories include local directories for your state or province, town, chamber of commerce, etc.

Getting listed in directories is generally a straightforward process. Usually they have an "add" button either on the home page or within each category. If possible, find the category of your product or service and add your site from there. It will not appear in the directory until your site has been reviewed and approved, which can take anywhere from a few hours to several months

Online advertising

Every day we are bombarded with images, sounds, and other inducements to buy — advertisements on billboards, in newspapers, on TV and radio and, most irritating of all, unasked for and generally unwanted email messages.

But we must admit that mass advertising does work or else companies trying to sell you their goods and services wouldn't use it. We've all been influenced to make a purchasing decision by information we have been given in one form or another. The advent of email promotion has also made mass marketing a cheap and not particularly difficult option because it is aimed at a mass audience where a 1 percent or 2 percent response rate from hundreds of thousands of people will result in enormous sales. Marketing your cottage is not quite in this league, but some of the same basic principles apply nonetheless.

For a moment, let's go back to the circus coming to town. If you stick your "Circus Coming" poster on a wall in the town center, it might be seen by people who shop in the town center; if it's stuck on a tree in the park, children may notice and ask their parents about it; if you manage to get a friend to pin it up on a notice board at work, it may be ignored because most of the people who work there don't have children and are not interested in circuses.

What this tells us is that advertising that is not deliberately targeted is random, a little like trying to hit a dartboard while blindfolded. Therefore, before you start you will need to identify your target audience

Choosing where you will advertise your property requires careful planning and budgeting. If you already own your cottage and advertise it on the Internet, you'll have experienced the upsurge of online vacation rental advertisers vying for your potentials customers. Here are a couple of examples:

> We would like to List your property on our new site!!! A Vacation Rental.com Affiliated with Another Vacation Rental.com 1 Year Half Price — Be the #1 Listing in Many Areas $44.50 — 100 percent Satisfaction Guaranteed!! No fees, no commission, direct owner contact.

> A Rental Calendar, Email collection and up to 8 photos. Don't hesitate, we are adding listings, but most of all — we are attracting prospective renters — A week empty is money gone forever ... $$$ Daily hits are at 34,000 — Multiple Property Discounts.

Reading between the lines here, being the "#1 Listing in Many Areas" probably means you are the only listing in your area. And what exactly does "100% Satisfaction Guaranteed!!" mean anyway?

We are anxious to build our inventory in your area. We are offering this promotion for the next 100 homeowners. Sign up for three months and you will get nine months free. That's right. 12 full months for $105.00. There is no better deal on the Internet. Please read our promo below.

If you are tempted by ads like these, have a close look at the site first and ask a few questions:

- In how many countries are their listings? They may have thousands of hits a day, but if those are not targeted hits — people actually looking for a cottage to rent in your part of the world — then the statistics are not worth a great deal.

- When did they last update the site? A recent look at a top-rated site on Google showed a list of late availability from the previous year. If you are paying for a listing on any site, you are entitled to have the site updated regularly.

- How easy is it for a prospective customer to find your property? Imagine yourself as a potential renter and go searching. If you get put off by a site, you can be sure that others will too.

- Where do they advertise? Posting a site on the Internet may not be enough to capture a target audience. If it is a more localized site, i.e., just listing properties in your tourist region, they may also advertise in local papers, tourism literature, etc.

Tempting as some of these offers may seem, careful vetting and research will pay dividends, helping you to keep your marketing within budget. One property owner who rents his vacation home year-round and has a high level of out-of-season rentals, offers this advice:

"When you plan how you will market your property, decide how much you want to spend on marketing and stick to it. It is just too easy to succumb to Internet advertising offering 'exclusive deals.' Put yourself in renters' shoes and search the web for a vacation rental in your area. Look at the sites that come to the top of the search engines. These are the ones who spend time marketing themselves and will offer the most value for you. Just think how easy it must be for some of these vacation rental operators to get a website up, find a database of cottage owners, and email them all. After asking for anything between $35 and $200 to list your cottage, put up a few photos and a description, they do nothing more. Let's face it. They don't make money from people going to the site to find a property — they make their money from us owners. So, where is the incentive for them to market any further?!"

If you are spending your money on advertising, make sure that money is going to work for you.

Wherever you decide to advertise, monitor it carefully to see what works and what doesn't. If you use an inquiry form for each call or email you receive, collect information on how they found you. At the end of the season, you can analyze which method produced the most interest and worked most effectively for you.

Rental listing sites

This type of site is simply an advertising medium. You pay a fee and the site staff places your cottage on a web page, giving your contact details. Most have an availability facility that you can update when you take a booking.

Expect to pay between $35 and $100 for a listing with an advertising-only site. With such a range it is a good idea to make a list of what your requirements are and shortlist those advertisers that meet them. Some criteria you may consider:

- Link popularity

- Ease of navigation, clarity, and organization of listing

- An availability calendar function

- Initial cost and additional costs for updating

- Late availability and special offers

- Number of photos and amount of detail allowed

As previously mentioned, there are a lot of sites offering advertising deals, all vying for your business. Take some time to look at some of the more popular ones, navigate their sites, contact some of their cottage advertisers and draw your own conclusions. Check if they have up-to-date information — websites that are not updated often enough annoy many visitors.

Link popularity

Take some time to find out how popular an advertising site is. There is an easy way of doing this by using a link popularity tool. Simply put, link popularity refers to the total number of links or "votes" that a search engine has found for a website. This lets you compare different sites to see how popular each one is by counting how many times it appears in the major search engines.

Try www.marketleap.com. When you get to the home page, click on Link Popularity Check, which takes you to a page where you can type in the web addresses (URLs) of vacation rental sites and find how many links they have to other sites. The more links, the greater the chance of people finding your listing.

Ease of navigation

Most readers will have spent time looking for things on websites. Whether it is a book on Amazon.com, an obscure collectible, or a piece of information for a research project, the process is much the same. You will get onto the site and want to find the product as quickly as possible. Imagine you are a customer and make a list of your "wants" for a cottage vacation. Using criteria such as location, size, price, etc, go onto the website of each agency you are considering and see what happens. How easy is it to find what you want? Then change your criteria and do this again. The results of this exercise should give you an indication of how hard the site designer has worked to meet the needs of visitors to the site.

This is a personal observation, but I am irritated by sites that have only a search function. I want to view all the properties they have, not be restricted by having to give the dates of travel or to narrow down a specific region.

Availability calendar

The vast majority of visitors to a rental website will want to know there and then if it is available for the period they require. Check to see if the site has an easy-to-follow availability calendar for each property. Most agencies offer their owner clients the facility to update their own calendar. Ask how this works and make sure you can update your availability for any time period, not just for the current year.

Cost

Having set your budget for advertising, you'll want the listing site's costing structure clearly stated so you can add this to your cash flow forecast. Most sites charge a standard fee for initial setup that will include text and a certain number of photographs. You will want to know what additional charges there are for:

- Posting additional photographs
- A link to your own website
- Changes to your listing after initial setup
- Listing your property as "Featured"
- Inclusion in a property finder or late availability section
- Special features

Some sites you look at may offer additional features that make them more attractive. Some have a section where rental customers can email and state their requirements generally, rather than by contacting each owner. This means you can access the list of people looking for property and contact them yourself with any special offer you may have.

A late availability section is an advantage for selling remaining weeks in the summer, perhaps due to cancellation. You want people looking for a last-minute rental to be able to find you quickly and easily. How well does the rental site do this?

When you have looked at each of these features, fill in the Rental Agency Comparison Chart on the CD-ROM to examine the similarities and differences.

PRINT ADVERTISING

Developing your website (and linking to create maximum exposure) is relatively inexpensive, but other forms of advertising can drain your budget very quickly. Classified advertising in newspapers and magazines is probably the most expensive form of advertising, and you would need to consider it very carefully before parting with your money.

Once you have a website up and running, you may receive unsolicited calls from a newspaper's advertising department offering highly discounted rates for a series of ads. Before being tempted, figure out how many weeks' rental you would have to sell in order to pay for that advertising — that is, what it takes to recoup the money. This is what your marketing budget is all about. If you have a clearly defined amount for advertising, it is much easier to be firm when responding to a heavy sales pitch!

If you do decide to try out this type of advertising, analyze the response. This will give you a clear indication of how well it worked. For example, if you spent $350 on a series of ads and this results in three weeks' rental yielding $4,500, this may appear to offer value for money. However, if the three weeks' rental could just as easily have been obtained through your annual subscription to a rental listing site at $50, perhaps it is not such a good deal after all.

The up-front costs of developing a website will be quickly covered by the return as the site gets exposure, whereas a couple of one-off ads are "here today, in the garbage tomorrow."

CREATING YOUR OWN LITERATURE

It will certainly help your marketing efforts if you have promotional literature to leave in your cottage or to hand out at trade shows or your chamber of commerce stand. A leaflet or tri-fold brochure that has good photos, a brief and attractive description, and your contact details can promote your property really well. You can then leave these in tourist offices and in local stores and gas stations — in fact, anywhere a visiting tourist may stop. This is a great tool to have for the off-season when you want to attract potential customers who may be looking to rent a property at short notice. In addition, it's a great way of showcasing your place to renters if they have just seen a small ad or a brief description on a website.

You may find that your local chamber of commerce tourist office exhibits at tourism and vacation shows and will include your leaflet in their display material. They might want you to become a member for this, but as the cost of doing so is relatively low, and the opportunities for wider marketing much higher, the benefits should outweigh the costs.

With relatively inexpensive desktop publishing software, you can easily create a professional-looking tri-fold leaflet. Alternatively, seek out a reasonably priced graphic designer, perhaps from a small local firm. Although significantly more expensive than the do-it-yourself option, you will have a professional product that will present your property in a quality manner. Either way, you must also consider printing costs.

What to put in a leaflet

There is limited space in a leaflet to include all the information that will encourage potential guests to call you. You will also be competing with many other resorts, cottages, and accommodations vying for that out-of-season customer, so you have to make an impact.

Photographs

Select good quality photographs — at least one of the exterior, a couple of interior shots, and perhaps one featuring an activity.

Remember you are portraying images of what you want your guests to experience, so choose those images that are more evocative. A warmly colored photo of a log fire, or a chair with a book and a glass of wine, will evoke more feelings and desire than a stark shot of your living room, however well furnished and appointed it is. Similarly, an image of someone fishing from the dock in the sunset will be more memorable than a plain image of the waterfront.

You don't necessarily need to use the photos you have on your website. What often happens is that someone sees your leaflet and then looks up your website to find out more. If you have simply put your brochure on the website, they will be disappointed. However, if you use different pictures and text, visitors to your website will stay longer as you are giving them additional information.

You will need photos of a much higher resolution for print material than those required for a website. If you are using a designer, he or she should be able to advise you on the technicalities.

Text

As with photographs, the words you use to describe your cottage should stimulate the emotions. Use feeling words such as *relaxing*, *warmth*, *comfort*, and *peace*; visual expressions such as *a night sky filled with a million stars*; and "hearing" words and phrases such as *the haunting call of a loon*, or *listening to the sound of pure silence*. This method of emotive writing has been shown to appeal to the broadest range of people and will have more impact than basic descriptions of a cottage. Compare the two examples below:

Imagine a long weekend away from the noise and bustle of the city. Settling in comfort and warmth in front of a blazing log fire, glass of wine in hand, looking forward to a break filled with as much relaxation or activity as you want. No streetlights to spoil the magnificence of a vast starlit sky, or sound of traffic to intrude on the peace. Come and experience it all in an idyllic waterfront setting.

We offer weekend breaks in our three-bedroom vacation rental in the Upper Peninsula.

Of course you'll need to include some information on the facilities offered, but these details can be listed on the back page rather than making them the main feature of the leaflet. You might also mention local places of interest, seasonal activities, and brief descriptions of any themed packages you offer. There is an example of a simple cottage leaflet design on the CD.

Rates

If you include your rates in your brochure, make sure you state the season and year for each price band. This way, you won't get a customer claiming a rate you had on a leaflet they picked up the previous year. For example:

November 1, 2006 – June 1, 2007 (excluding holidays)	$950 per week
Christmas & New Year's 2006/07	$1,400 per week
Spring break 2007	$1,400 per week
Long weekends in low season only (e.g., 4 p.m. Fri May 21 – 4 p.m. Mon May 24)	$650 (for 4 persons), $60 per additional person

Printing your brochure

If you are designing the brochure yourself and printing on high-quality paper on a good color printer, you will have a marketing tool created at low cost that looks attractive and well produced. You can also look locally for a small office services company that will print your leaflet inexpensively on a digital printer. This means you can have as many or as few as you want. It also allows you to change your leaflet with the seasons. You can then send a fall brochure describing hiking and biking, and a winter wonderland leaflet extolling the delights of renting your property for a short break in the winter, to people who stayed in the summer and to all those you have on your mailing list; don't forget to include your Christmas and New Year's rates in this as well.

Distribution and mailing lists

Send copies of your brochure to your local chamber of commerce tourist office. Leave some in the rental property, and ask guests to take them for their friends. Give a dozen or so to your family and business colleagues, and put them on your notice board at work. In short, if you have gone to the trouble of producing your brochures, don't relegate them to a desk drawer — get them in front of as many people as possible.

Throughout the year you will receive many requests for information on your listing that don't result in a booking. Just because people don't come back to you doesn't mean they won't in the future. They obviously liked the look of your property or they wouldn't have made an inquiry in the first place. These inquirers become your mailing list, which is a very valuable database. In sales terms, people who have already expressed an interest in a product, even if they don't buy on the first occasion, are hot leads and should be the first to be contacted when you have any new marketing material prepared or "special offers" to promote.

> "I enquired about a privately owned cabin for a vacation in Fernie, BC, a while back. We didn't go, but every so often we get an email with an offer for the new season, or information on special deals. It always looks so enticing that when we do get to go to BC, that's where we will stay. I'm planning to do an email letter about our place, along the same lines as the Fernie property."

PRIVACY OF INFORMATION

There is no single law in the US that provides a comprehensive treatment of data protection or privacy issues. Most are geared to federal databases and not to small businesses collecting information on their customers. However, in Canada, if you keep personal information on other people for business purposes, you are obliged to comply with the provisions of the Personal Information

Protection and Electronic Documents Act. You don't have to be a registered business to comply with the act as the definition of organization includes a "person" as a collector of information. Compliance means following the guidelines of the act and making sure information is collected and disclosed in certain ways. More information is available at www.privcom.gc.ca.

A professional approach to the data your have on your clients is vital to retaining their confidence. Be open about what you will do with their private information, and always ask before you use it for any marketing purposes.

MONITOR YOUR MARKETING

Whatever form of advertising and marketing you choose, it is imperative that you keep a record of how effective each method is. Always ask people where they first heard of your property. That way you can analyze just how well each marketing opportunity is working for you. If people come via your website, ask them what they thought of it — did they find all the information they wanted, and was there anything else that would have made it more user friendly? Start chatting and glean as much information as you can. If you don't gather this data, you'll never know what's working best, and having this information will save you money in the long run. Keep a database of all the people who have asked for information, or have rented with you before. Don't forget, whenever you produce a new leaflet, or if there is something new on your website, let them know.

FREQUENT GUEST INCENTIVE

"In marketing, I've seen only one strategy that can't miss and that is to market to your best customers first, your best prospects second, and the rest of the world last."

— *John Romero*

Your repeat guests will probably be your best advocates, and it is a great gesture to reward them for singing the praises of your vacation home. Have your own version of a frequent flyers' club — give it a name such as "Friends of the Cottage." Offer these guests an incentive for telling other people what a great place you have by giving them a percentage discount, maybe 10 percent for each booking they generate through their marketing on your behalf. The discount could be redeemable for off-season weekends and could accumulate to a maximum 50 percent off, for instance. For your most prolific marketers, the offer of completely free weekends will encourage them further. You just decide on the level of discount, call it a "club," and wait for the referrals to flow.

At the beginning of each season, contact all your previous season's guests and offer them first call on the high-season weeks. Keep in touch with them year-round too, with special offers or late availability deals.

NEWSLETTER

A useful idea for keeping people interested is a seasonal newsletter. This can include details of any updating you have done to the cottage, upcoming events and activities, and any special offers you may have. If your area has events such as arts weeks, craft fairs, dogsled derbies, winter carnivals, etc., advertise these within your newsletter, and perhaps offer a special rate. For example:

Arts Weekend

Enjoy the delights of the Haliburton Arts Week from your base at Lakeside Cottage. Enjoy a leisurely breakfast in the morning before heading out to view the talents and skills of our county's best artisans. On your arrival at the cottage, you'll find maps and leaflets describing the best route to follow to see a variety of artists and craftspeople with suggestions for lunch stops. Return to the cottage in the evening for a barbecue and hot tub and a good night's sleep before continuing your studio visits on Sunday.

> Arts Weekend rate: $400 — Friday, September 16th (4 p.m. check-in) — Sunday, September 18th (11 a.m. checkout).

There are some excellent newsletter templates for different times of the year offered online, which are really easy to use. Many offer a free 30-day trial so you can test to see how effective they are for you.

OPEN-HOUSE WEEKEND

Prospective renters will often want to have a look at a property before they make a firm booking. This is a great idea as you get to meet prospective renters and they get to see what they are spending their money on. Make sure you, or a representative, are there to meet them as this is an excellent opportunity to show off the best parts of your cottage and point out features that may not be so easily explained on your website or in a brochure. It is not a good idea at any time to give the address of your vacation home to any potential renter without collecting their identification information.

A great idea is to offer open days in your low season when people can visit the property, meet you, ask questions about activities, etc. This gives you the chance to meet your guests in advance, which certainly helps in the vetting process. You are there in person to show off your vacation home at its best — make sure it is spotlessly clean, the beds are freshly made up, and there is a welcoming smell of coffee together with the wood fire crackling merrily away. These first impressions count for such a lot. The aim of an open day is not only to fill your rental calendar for the summer, but also to show visitors what a great place it would be to come for a short break out-of-season.

"We went to an open house at a log home manufacturer one November. We'd seen so many pictures of these places that, after a while, they all seemed the same. To actually walk into one that was set up as a show home, smell fresh coffee and donuts, see the richness of the logs, and hear firsthand about the manufacturing process, was so good. It was such a great idea that we modeled our first open house for would-be renters on it. We took about half our next year's bookings on that day, and booked winter weekend breaks as well. The model really worked!"

Advertise the open-house days/weekends on your website together with suggestions for taking the opportunity to visit some other attractions in the area. Ask interested people to email you with their name and address so you can get some idea of numbers to expect. If you know of other rental owners in the area who would be interested in having an open house on the same day, you could offer quite a unique day out. If there is sufficient interest, the competition created by doing this with others shouldn't affect your uptake.

Have coffee and juice available, and maybe some cookies and donuts. Place a donation box next to them so you can collect for your favorite charity at the same time.

Have your paperwork and a calendar available so you can take bookings on the day, perhaps offering some incentive — maybe a discount — for low-season bookings. Make sure you have copies of your rental agreement available, and expect to take deposits there and then, offering a cooling off period of a few days.

Your advertisement for the open house could be something along the lines of:

Thinking of renting a vacation home in the area, and not sure where to start looking?

Come up to our open house on Saturday, October 22nd. Look around our beautiful home and get a feel for this great vacation spot. Make a day of it, and explore the wonderful area — it's great at this time of year. Sign our guest book, and if you book a short break out-of-season, or at a later date, you'll receive a 10 percent discount.

Marketing successfully means working at it regularly. Set an hour or two aside each week when you will concentrate on a new marketing activity, and stick with it. Keep in mind that it is not good enough to put up a website, print a few leaflets, and place an ad in the paper every so often. That complacency will not find the people and new guests you need to make your rental business profitable. If you want this to work, then you have to as well! And all that work will pay dividends in increased rentals, profits, and lots of satisfaction!

10
RENTAL MANAGEMENT AGENCIES

Although managing your own vacation home rental can be reward-ing and, in some ways, economical, it is very time-consuming and demands a high degree of attention for it to be successful. This is where rental management companies can offer a great alternative or become an additional tool in your marketing plan.

Bear in mind when you make this decision that you will lose a significant amount of your income in commission.

TYPES OF AGENCIES AND SERVICES

There are many advantages to relinquishing all the hassle to an agency; however, one disadvantage is that the agency may insist on having the property fully available for renting for a certain num-ber of weeks, including the peak season and other holiday periods. It may simply not be worth their while to spend money advertising and marketing your property if you're going to spend a lot of time there yourself. This means you may not be able to use the property for your own family or at the spur of the moment. The rental management agency's contract should cover owner occupancy, so make sure you agree on this before signing it.

Agencies have two types of customers: the owner, for whom they deliver a range of rental management services; and the renter, to whom they supply information and reservation facilities. The agency that represents your property should not only deal promptly with your queries and concerns but must also provide excellent service to the people who want to rent. If it doesn't do that, you won't get the customers you need to rent your vacation home. Good agencies should pay equal attention to both owners and renters, and if they are acting efficiently on your behalf you should expect a high level of service from them.

Booking agencies

The upsurge of demand for self-catering-style vacations has led to growth in the number of rental agencies now established in North America. Many concentrate on a single region, with perhaps a few properties outside their immediate area. The larger agencies cover a wider geographical area and have many properties on offer ranging from basic cabins to the luxury end of the market. A number of companies offer a booking service only. They will inspect the property, advertise it on their website, process contracts and rental agreements, and collect rental fees and security deposits. However, they do not have the facility to manage rental changeovers, check for damage and cleanliness, or respond to any problems that may arise during rental.

Full-service agencies

Full-service agencies will undertake the same tasks as booking-only agencies but will also offer additional services, either through their own resources or by affiliation with other companies. Examples of these services are guest care, maintenance and emergency repair, linen rental, cleaning and changeover, bicycle and equipment rental, etc. Owners may be able to choose from booking services only, booking plus changeover service, or a complete rental and property management service. This means a vacation home owner can be completely confident that one company is carrying out every aspect of the rental/property management package if that level of service is required.

If you are an absent owner — perhaps living in a different state or country, this would be a useful option for you to have.

"We were using an agency to rent our place and thought they covered everything. The cabin was checked between rentals, and all seemed OK. Then, last August, I was just about to start a bicycle race in BC, when my cell phone rang. It was the renters in my cottage complaining that the water pump hadn't come on after a power outage. They had called the agency who said it wasn't their problem, and suggested they call me. I was mad, the renters weren't too happy, and that ended my relationship with that agency. In retrospect, I hadn't read through my responsibilities thoroughly enough, so to a certain extent it was my fault — I should have thought through what I needed from an agency before signing up. From my viewpoint, I live too far away to do much with the cottage myself, so I need a full-service agency that can help with all my needs in the future."

With this in mind, it's really important to know what you expect from an agency. If you simply want them to advertise, set up rental agreements, handle money, and take away the hassles of marketing and deal with incoming inquiries, then most of the agencies currently advertising on the Internet will be able to do that for you. If you live some distance away and you don't have a reliable person to manage your cottage in your absence nor do you relish the idea of troubleshooting while your renters are there, you will need to ask potential agencies some searching questions to establish if they are right for you.

When you start to look for an agency, prepare a list of questions. In this way you can be sure you are asking each agency the same questions and can compare the answers. Ask for their information package so you can do some initial comparisons on their commission rates, for example. You shouldn't expect any agency to give you an estimate of rental potential without visiting your cottage, nor should they begin marketing it without a thorough inspection. Many different things determine a market rate, and it would be unfair to ask for such an estimate, sight unseen. You may already have a good idea of what to expect from looking at the agencies' rates; however, keep in mind that some of those rates include a booking fee that is payable by renters. Their information package should tell you how the agency operates, where they advertise and market their services, and what experience they have managing rental properties. It should also include testimonials from current owners registered with them.

It is easy to set up an agency — collecting commission by managing vacation rentals can seem like an easy way to generate income. This is why it is important to research carefully.

Different states and provinces may have regulatory requirements for agencies. For example, those based in Ontario are regulated by the Travel Industry Act and must be registered with TICO, the Travel Industry Council of Ontario. This protects consumers' money and indicates the agencies' professional status. In some areas agencies are regulated by real estate boards.

The Vacation Rental Managers Association (VRMA) can be found at www.vrma.com. VRMA members represent the leading short-term property management firms in North America, and with over 600 member firms in the United States, Canada, Mexico, and the Caribbean, they represent approximately 125,000 rental homes. This is probably a good start in finding an agency that adheres to professional standards.

Of course, word of mouth is arguably the best recommendation, and if you know of other owners who use an agency, ask for their testimonials.

Agency rates

Agency rates vary, though not as widely as it may seem from a first glance at their rate sheets or websites. Some charge a flat commission rate that is payable only when the property is rented; a few have an initial setup fee and advertising charge, with a variable administration fee per week; and most charge renters a fee for booking. Commission rates vary from 12 percent to 45 percent, so there is considerable variation in rates. Doing your homework thoroughly will indicate where you will get the best value while remembering that the old adage also applies: "You get what you pay for."

Viewing

When you contact agencies, they will want to arrange a viewing of your property. Even if you are inviting several agencies, expect them all to take photographs and carefully question you on the facilities and amenities available, and any restrictions you may want to impose. When you appoint the agency, they will already have the photographs and information, so they won't need to revisit. Make sure the property looks its best. Photographs will capture how your property looks that day. If the weather is poor, or the season prevents the best exterior shots from being taken, have available a selection of your own best photographs.

Well in advance of the viewing, prepare a detailed sheet listing room dimensions, bed configurations, additional features, and kitchen appliances. Some agencies will provide you with a form on which you can complete all the relevant details.

Additional services

Agencies often have a menu of services they can offer in addition to marketing your cottage — changeover, meet and greet, cleaning, maintenance, etc. Some will also assist in supplying linens and making beds, which is a bonus for attracting overseas visitors.

Smaller agencies

Operating in specific areas, smaller agencies may offer a more personal approach as they are only representing a small number of properties. You will need to weigh the advantage of this against the wider presence offered by the bigger agencies.

CHOOSING AN AGENCY

Good agencies will freely provide you with references from their clients, so look at their websites and property lists and ask for contact information of owners you would like to speak with. Select properties in your rental price bracket, but also take the time to talk to people who have rental homes at other ends of the spectrum. This will give you an idea of how the agency operates. Don't just rely on the testimonials on the site. Although these are likely to be genuine, they will be biased towards the positive and you want to find out what other clients don't like as well as what they do. That way, you'll get a balanced view of the agency, which will enable you to make a really informed decision.

With growing competition, agencies need to offer top-class customer service to generate good feedback from renters, and consequently generate more potential renters through word-of-mouth recommendations.

Ask plenty of questions to establish their views on the things that matter to you. These are just some suggestions — you may think of others:

- Does the agency respond promptly to your queries? If they are not quick in responding to you, how quick will they be in getting back to potential renters for your cottage?

- What are their hours of operation? Most people want to book holidays during evenings and weekends — is the agency open at these times?

- Do they have a toll-free number?

- Is the voice-mail message friendly and welcoming?

- Is their website easy to navigate?

- Are the availability listings unambiguous?

- Will they organize general maintenance and repairs, and how will that be billed?

- What do they do to attract people during the low season?

- What can they do for you if you have last-minute availability (for example, if a renter cancels)? Some agencies have a late availability feature so that customers can find out what is currently available for the time that they want.

- What is their cancellation policy?

- What happens in the case of an emergency when guests are occupying the cottage?

- Where do they advertise?

- How do they screen guests?

- What does the agency's rental agreement cover? You should be able to place conditions on your rental that are included in the agency's rental agreement. Guests of your vacation property must comply with these policies, which may be in regards to minimum age, maximum occupants, composition (families, singles), smoking, and pets.

- How do they deal with damage beyond normal wear and tear?

So how do you make that final selection? Once again, look at the results of your Internet search. Which agencies are repeatedly showing up at the top of the search engines? Do they have a presence at local and national home and vacation shows — an important showcase for your property? Decide what criteria are important to you, then draw up a table in Word or Excel with these criteria listed across the top and names of the agencies in the left-hand column. Don't forget to include the website of the agency — or perhaps you can hyperlink the agency name. A sample table is included on the CD-ROM.

THE CONTRACT

All the professionally run agencies will ask you to sign a contract that lays out the responsibilities of the agency and the owner. Contracts will differ in certain respects but will mostly cover the following:

Duration of agreement

This states how long you are contracted to the agency. It may be for a predetermined period such as six months or a year, or it may be terminated at any time with advance notice, a period such as 60 days. A typical term agreement would look like this:

> The term of the Agreement shall commence on _____ and shall terminate upon sixty (60) days after advance written notice given by either party. Termination of this agreement does not invalidate any existing rental agreements made by THE AGENT on THE OWNER's behalf. THE OWNER shall continue to be responsible, or shall cause to be completed, all obligations or expenses incurred hereunder by THE AGENT. In the event this agreement is terminated, or the property is sold, THE OWNER shall honor all confirmed reservations.

Clearly the agency wants to cover itself in the event of the property owner selling the property or moving to another agency. Generally, this type of clause will appear at the top of the rental management contract, and it is one you will need to consider carefully.

Responsibilities

Most contracts will list a series of responsibilities for the owner and the agent. The agency's responsibilities are varied and may cover all or some of the following:

- General services
- Advertising and marketing
- Preparation of rental agreements (and termination of an agreement with a renter, if necessary)
- Bookkeeping and/or accounting services
- Collection and refund of security deposits
- Security and maintenance of records
- Communication with property owner

- Handling of subcontracted services

The owner also has responsibilities and these should be clearly identified within the agreement. The clauses may cover the following:

- Provision of furnishings and fittings that have been advertised as part of the property

- Maintenance and upkeep of the interior and exterior of the property

- Provision and maintenance of watercraft and recreational equipment that can be used by the renter

- Insurance and liability coverage

- Payment of utilities, additional heating, and telephone bills

- Communication with agent

- Owner's use of the property

In general, there should be no restrictions on your use of your vacation property; however, the contract may require that you give adequate notice. This is only fair if the agency is marketing your property and aiming at a specific rental period — they expect to get a return on their money and wouldn't appreciate you taking that period for yourself, especially if it's at the last minute. The following is an example of a clause relating to owners' occupancy of the property:

> Should OWNER fail to inform AGENT of OWNER'S occupancy of property, and should AGENT obtain a rental for the property which could not be accommodated as a result of OWNER'S occupancy, then OWNER shall be responsible for any and all costs associated with that rental, including but not limited to rental commissions.

You may be able to negotiate your own clause regarding your proposed usage of the property; however, bear in mind that the agency will have marketing, advertising, and administration costs associated with your property, and if their use of it is limited, it may not be worth their while to act as your agent.

Exclusivity

Rental agencies would prefer you have an exclusive contract with them, as a number of issues can inevitably arise if more than one agency is involved. When more than one agency is advertising and marketing a property, double booking is, of course, a major issue, and communication has to be timely and accurate. A nonexclusive contract is not for the owner who wants rentals handled at arm's length, as it would require him or her to be heavily involved in all potential bookings.

Similarly, most agencies would prefer their owners did not do any marketing themselves. This can confuse renters as they are not sure who to contact if they have seen the property on an agency website and also on the owner's site. Also, you may end up advertising a lower price than the agency, who do need to make a commission, but this is ill-advised. Vacation renters are savvy people who will probably see a property everywhere it is advertised, and they will not be happy if they see it offered on a rental agency site at a higher price than the owner is presenting. Although this is not illegal in any way, it does not show the agency in a good light.

Some agencies will charge an additional percentage if there is a nonexclusive contract.

Agent's fees

The contract should clearly state the agent's fee structure, including any setup fee and subsequent commission rate, administration fees, and reservation charges made to the renter. You should find out when the funds will be paid to you. This may depend on the regulation for your state or province and whether your agency is licensed and regulated by a real estate or travel industry body. On this note, it is important that you check that your agency has the appropriate state or provincial licensing.

Using a rental agency does take the hassle out of managing the marketing and booking of your property, and you will pay a significant price for this service. So, if you decide to go this route, do a lot of research to find the right one for you. It could be a relationship that lasts for many years with many happy renters, or you could find yourself with empty weeks and a commitment to a rental program that is doing nothing for you.

11
MANAGING YOUR PROPERTY YOURSELF

If you are seriously planning a rental business rather than something more casual, you will need to consider how you will handle the management of your property between rentals, as well as having someone available locally in case of problems. If your property is being left unoccupied for any length of time, it is normally a requirement of your insurance policy that it is checked regularly anyway.

One owner's experience would have been immensely costly if he had not had his property manager checking the vacation home on a regular basis.

A leaking pipe in an upstairs bathroom caused $10,000 worth of damage, and it had only been leaking for a day or two. Still, it took two weeks to dry, and three weeks' work to repair the damage to drywall, carpets, and paintwork. Fortunately, it was covered by the owner's rental insurance policy, but only because he was able to prove it was checked regularly. A salutary tale! Having a commercial rental policy also meant insurance coverage for the loss of rental income.

So, there are a number of issues here — and many of them depend on where you are usually located in relation to your vacation property. If you live hundreds of miles away, you will not be in a position to be caretaker/maintenance person/cleaner/yard worker to your rental guests. Nor will the property be monitored and checked while it's empty. However, there are many vacation home owners who have the benefit of having their cottage or cabin close by — even on the same property as their main residence. If that is the case, property management may not be an issue for you, providing you never plan on being absent during the rental season.

PROS AND CONS OF SELF-MANAGEMENT

One argument against employing a property manager is that you will save money if you do the job yourself. This may be true if you believe you are the only one who can appreciate what needs to be done by way of general maintenance and minor repairs. Sure, if that is the case, you've got the property management side of the business covered. However, if you are a new owner or have decided for the first time that the rental opportunities are too good to miss, you should weigh up the costs involved in taking on this task against the benefits of peace of mind and more time for yourself and your family.

Let's say you have rented four single weeks and two 2-week periods in the summer, a total of eight weeks. You'll have six changeovers to do — six trips up from the city to do the cleaning, check for damage, and do any minor maintenance, yard work, pool management, etc. That is quite a cost in terms of both your time and your money (consider travel time and travel expenses), and you may only have three to four hours in which to do all these things before the new renters arrive to enjoy your property as you make the drive back. And then what happens if there is a problem in the middle of the week? The septic backs up; there's a frozen pipe during a winter rental; the water stops running. Are you able to drop everything, drive straight up to your property, and arrange for it to be fixed?

"We rented a large place one February for a weekend. It was a palatial home rather than a basic cabin, and we certainly never expected anything to go wrong. The day after we arrived, I noticed a really unpleasant smell in the shower room. Looking into the shower stall I saw brown liquid coming up into the shower tray! It smelled like sewage, and sure enough, that's what it was. We rang the owner who was totally at a loss as to what to do. He just told me he'd never had the problem before, so it must have been us that caused it. When we asked when the septic was last emptied, he said he wasn't aware it needed emptying — he'd bought the property the previous year, and no one had mentioned he should need to do that! He wouldn't come out and, as it was a weekend, said he didn't know of any plumbers. We'd have to put up with it ...

"There were ten in our party, so it sure made the rest of the weekend difficult. I couldn't believe someone would rent out a place without having someone available to troubleshoot problems or just give some reassurance that it was being dealt with."

Some owners rent out their properties from Sunday to Saturday, allowing them an entire day to do the turnaround. This works, but not from a profitability viewpoint, as you will be losing six days' worth of rental every six weeks. It also means that guests feel they have missed out on having a full weekend, which may reduce the attraction of your property to potential renters.

You are on call throughout the period of the rental, and you must be very well organized if you are to handle any problems that may occur. In winter this is particularly important. A spell of really cold weather can freeze pipes that had never been a problem before, so before offering a winter rental, make sure you check everything is working in your cottage before your guests arrive.

Think of a worst-case scenario, and ask yourself if you are fully prepared to deal with that. If you are, then self-management is the way to go.

MANAGEMENT OPTIONS

There are several options for management of your cottage that you might consider. Each one has its own benefits and drawbacks, and it's important to weigh these up and make a decision based on a set of criteria. These could include:

- *Cost.* What do you realistically expect to pay?

- *Confidence.* How comfortable are you with leaving the day-to-day running of your property to someone else?

- *Trust.* It's really important that you feel your manager is completely trustworthy.

Table 1 compares some of the advantages and disadvantages of various management options.

Let's say you have decided to employ a third party to look after your property when you are not there. There are several possibilities here. First, you might be lucky enough to have friendly neighbors who are also good at repairs and would be delighted to take on a part-time job looking after your place. This can work extremely well providing —

- they are happy to be on call whenever you have guests in your cottage;

- they are willing to check on the place when it's left empty; and

- you trust that they will be reliable and meet the commitments you make to your guests.

UK-based owners of an Ontario cottage found a local couple who were delighted to take on the care of their cottage and do a great job of it. The owners made sure from the outset that it was a proper business arrangement with a monthly fee covering a specific range of tasks, and it has worked so well that the owners have now bought another cottage locally and their caretakers are looking after that one as well.

TABLE 1
PROS AND CONS OF MANAGEMENT OPTIONS

Caretaker	Advantages	Disadvantages
Yourself	• You know your property intimately • You get to check your property yourself	• Time-consuming • Traveling costs • Can be stressful
Neighbors	• Know you and your cottage • Familiar with the area • Helpful and friendly • Low cost	• Can affect friendship • May not be willing to be "on call" • Enthusiasm may wane quickly
Local handyman	• More businesslike footing • Has skills to take on maintenance and repairs	• Can be unreliable • May take on too much
Property management company	• Has skilled workers experienced in all aspects of property management • Professional service • Inspires confidence • Will offer contract-based work — more reliable • Will arrange for subcontractors if required	• Higher cost • May be inflexible and require more notice of changes

"It works because we explained clearly at the start what we expected, and the standards we required. They do a fantastic job, and it shows from the comments on cleanliness in our visitors' book."

It is clear that an arrangement with a neighbor must be conducted in a businesslike manner with an agreed-to fee — either a fixed monthly amount or a scale of charges depending on the work carried out (and that work can be substantial if you have a large property with a good parcel of land). Be aware that if the relationship is too casual, it just won't work: you will feel let down and you may even lose a friendship.

In many areas you will find advertisements for handyman services in the local papers, in gas stations, and on grocery store notice boards. Before taking on someone, make sure you get genuine testimonials from their clients — speaking to them directly if possible. Reliability is a key issue for vacation home owners. With often only a few hours between changeovers, you want to be confident that jobs will be done in a timely and professional manner and that the place will be ready in good time for the next guests. Make a list of all the tasks you want someone to do at your property. Once again, agree on a scale of charges or a set fee for all work undertaken, and ask for a professional invoice so that you have all the paperwork necessary for tax purposes.

There are many dedicated property management companies, particularly in popular tourist areas where numerous vacation rental properties are located. Once again, seek out testimonials from their customers, asking about the company's reliability and professionalism. Look for companies that provide a menu of their services and that clearly state their price structure. They will probably want to see your property and to discuss the extent of the work you want done before they give you a quote, so write down a list of tasks you expect them to be responsible for before you meet.

Create a list of all the jobs that are likely to be needed throughout the main rental period. Include even the minor (but just as important) ones, such as watering garden tubs and flower baskets, raking the horseshoe and fire pits, and cleaning the barbecue.

Many of the complaints we hear from renters concern the areas surrounding the vacation home looking unkempt and untidy. This doesn't mean the desert scrub familiar to Arizona enthusiasts, or the type of waterfront cottage on a rocky outcrop on Georgian Bay where the natural features are part of its beauty, but a property with landscaped areas that have been allowed to overgrow. If the outside of the property looks unloved, it's natural to assume that the inside will also reflect that lack of care. It's therefore important that whoever maintains your property doesn't try to cut corners in any way, and that they carry out your instructions to the letter.

"Our cottage sits on ten acres of woodland with over 1,000 feet of waterfront on the river. Approximately an acre of the land is grassed, and there is a horseshoe pit, a volleyball area, and a gated children's play area with a slide and sandbox. In the summer, we like to have plenty of flower baskets and tubs, and our guests just love it. However, all this maintenance has to be carried out regularly. We once tried asking our guests to water the outdoor flower tubs. That was a disaster as we found, after a two-week rental, our politely written note about watering was ignored. We now have a property management company that comes in weekly to cut the lawns and do general garden maintenance. Whenever possible it's all carried out on changeover day so our guests aren't disturbed.

If you do this yourself, then it would just be a part of your changeover schedule. If you have a local person acting as caretaker, make sure he or she is aware when you want the outdoor work carried out.

"Our river property is very secluded, and we understand our guests do take advantage of the seclusion! A UK-based journalist in an article for one of the London newspapers described his stay at The River House: 'In the heat of the day we'd all flop naked into our river.' There would have been a few embarrassed faces all round if our property management team had arrived to cut the lawn while the family was having their swim!"

It's not always possible to carry out maintenance in the few short hours between guests leaving and the next arriving. Make sure that your guests know if you have arranged for any repairs or maintenance to be carried out. For the short time they have your cottage, they want peace and quiet, not to be disturbed by mowers, trimmers, and in one case we know of, three days of tree felling! You should give notice in advance of yard work or other maintenance.

> "The team our property management company sends in looks good, which we like, as it comes across as professional. They wear company polo shirts with dark work pants, not jeans, and baseball caps with their logo. A minor point we know, but it just looks so much better than a bare-chested guy with cut-off denim shorts. Nothing against cut-offs, but they have their place, and we wouldn't want that in our backyard while we have paying guests enjoying their vacation. And the truck they drive is always clean and displays the company logo clearly. That's a useful security feature, as our guests know who it is when they arrive."

GENERAL MAINTENANCE

If you live a long way from your property and may not get there more than a couple of times a year, a reliable person to carry out general maintenance duties is a must. There's a whole range of tasks you can call on them to do — the following are just suggestions:

Spring

- Opening-up tasks
- Pest control
- Checking for any winter damage
- Spring cleaning
- Putting out docks

- Cleanup and preparation of watercraft
- Planting
- Flower basket and tub preparation
- Deck staining
- Yard cleanup

Summer

- Lawn care
- Tree and shrub pruning
- Tub and basket watering and maintenance
- Regular cleaning
- Beach raking

Fall

- Wood supply and stacking
- Removal of docks
- Winterizing and storing watercraft
- Winterizing property (if not year-round)
- Winterizing plants, shrubs, and tubs
- Raking and burning or disposal of leaves
- Rodent control
- Renovation, repairs, and construction

Winter

- Regular security and damage checks
- Plowing
- Clearance of roof and deck snow
- Festive holiday decorating

MEETING AND GREETING

Many owners either greet their guests personally or ask their care-taker or property manager to do so. This is a matter of personal preference, but whatever you decide to do, let your guests know what to expect on arrival. Guests often arrive after dark, and it is really important that they know where to find a key if there is nobody to meet them. The last thing you want is for your phone to be ringing at midnight, with an irate guest complaining there is no key where you said it would be! It's quite common practice to leave a key somewhere handy for your guests to find, or use a lock-box. If you decide to meet your guests after they arrive, it's a good idea to let them unpack and make themselves at home before you show up.

Many guests I spoke with said that they would really prefer to arrive on their own and explore the place themselves, not dutifully follow the owner around as he or she tells them his or her life his-tory. That would be fine if it were over coffee the following day and the renters had recovered from the trip up, but not on the day of arrival when all they want to do is open a bottle of wine, sit on the deck, and really relax.

"Some years ago, ten of us arrived from the UK on a late February afternoon for a touring vacation starting with three nights in a very large property. For anyone who has traveled back from Europe, you'll know that you feel pretty jaded after getting in at 4 p.m. EST (which is 9 p.m. back in the UK), queuing for immigration, wrestling the throngs in the baggage hall, waiting another hour in the rental car lineup, then hitting the highway in the height of the rush hour! We were beat! So the prospect of getting to this lux-ury villa, relaxing by the fire, even getting in the hot tub, was very appealing.

"We arrived almost as planned at 8 p.m. (1 a.m. UK time), to be met by the owner. I have no quarrel with peo-ple being proud of their homes and liking to show them off, but this bordered on the ridiculous. An hour and a half later, the owner was still explaining the heating system — that was after instructions on using the washer and dryer, dishwasher, and barbecue, how to operate the showers, where to find the cues for the snooker table, and what the optimum temperature of the hot tub was, and going through three pages of instructions of what not to do. I am all for a comprehensive guest guide that covers all eventualities — in fact, that is a must — but in this place there were notices wherever you looked, most of which started with 'DO NOT ': 'DO NOT touch this switch under any circumstances'; 'DO NOT take bedroom towels out to the hot tub'; 'DO NOT operate the dishwasher and the washing machine at the same time.' All good points, I'm sure, but labored nonetheless. By the time the owner had departed, we were all exhausted."

— *Cottage guests from England*

Think of the last time you bought a car, especially if it was a new one — you understand the urge to just get in and drive away. The last thing you want is the sales representative issuing reams of instructions on how to maximize fuel efficiency, change the windscreen wipers, and check water levels. You already know the specifications and probably have had a test drive, so all you need is a good manual and a phone number to call should you have any questions. The same goes for a vacation home.

I hear the chorus of "it's not the same — this is our property that we are giving over to strangers, and they need to know all the quirkier aspects of it." With good planning, a thoroughly written guest guide, good screening of prospective guests, and a commitment to why you are in this business, you should feel comfortable in at least letting them settle in for a couple of hours, or only spending a very short time with them on arrival. If you do want to show them around, we would suggest making it a very brief tour. Your guests just want you to go away so they can explore in their own time, perhaps wash up after a long journey, and as they are on holiday they'll be wanting to relax with a cold drink! So resist the temptation to regale them with stories of the last time the septic blocked up, or about the raccoons in the attic last summer. Put any warnings in the guest guide, make sure you send a copy for them to read before they arrive, have a prominently displayed copy in the cottage, ask them to sign to say they have read and understand the instructions, and leave them be. They will appreciate you, and your home, all the more for that.

CLEANING

I have met some vacation home owners who prepare their property at the beginning of the season and don't visit again until the end, relying on their guests to do the cleanup after their stay in readiness for the next guests. Naturally, standards vary. What is acceptable to one family or group may be uninhabitable to another, and whatever these standards may be, people are paying for their accommodation and will be expecting a certain level of cleanliness at the start of their stay. In general, even if renters leave the place clean and tidy (as they should if your rental agreement specifies it), don't expect it to be spotless. That is up to you, or whomever you employ to do the turnaround. If you use a cleaning company, make it clear what you expect them to do, and leave a checklist to cover all these things. A good property manager will go through this thoroughly before you sign a contract, and you'll then be covered should there be any complaints. See the suggested cleaning and changeover checklist included on the CD.

A sad story was told by a resort owner who was approached early one morning by a family asking if she had any cabins to rent. It being the height of summer, she only had a one-bedroom unit that was vacant for just one night. The story was that the family had booked a vacation rental on the same lake based on an advertisement on a website. They spoke to the owner who told them it was a clean and well-furnished place, had lovely waterfront, and was ideal for a family. They arrived late at night to find the property had not been cleaned after the last renters, which must have been a week or two previously, as the place had become overrun by mice. Worse was to come in the morning, after they had spent the night in the car. In the light of day, they saw the damage the mice had done to mattresses and pillows, and the bags of garbage that had been left inside the cottage. Compounding the situation was the inability to access the waterfront from the property, it being on the wrong side of the cottage road. The nearest public beach area was a considerable walk around the lake. For a family who had looked forward to their annual vacation to be so sadly disappointed and let down was a tragedy.

In some regions and in some types of vacation property, it is standard for a cleaning supplement to be added on the rental rate and for renters to leave the property in a tidy state (but not necessarily to clean it). In other, more remote areas, guests will be asked to leave the property in an "as found" condition so the changeover crew have a minimal amount to do, given that they only have a short time. Whatever your policy on end-of-rental cleaning, just make it absolutely clear to the rental party what you expect them to do. You can offer an optional cleaning service if you are given sufficient notice to book this with your property managers or cleaning company. A comprehensive cleaning checklist left in the guest guide leaves your renters in no doubt as to what is expected of them.

What is most important is that the property your guests enter at the start of their vacation is spotlessly clean and well maintained. That way, there can be no argument over the standard of cleaning.

COTTAGE SECURITY AND KEY ISSUES

I know a property owner who has a high occupancy level at a rental rate of over $3,000 per week and leaves his property keys in the barbecue. Another hangs her key on a branch of the "third tree left of the garage," which was OK until the tree branch came down in a storm, rendering her guest information invalid! Other favorite spots are under plant pots or painted rocks; on a hook in the shed; or simply, "under the doormat." In some areas this may be acceptable to owners simply because many of them still don't feel the need to lock up their property anyway. Sadly, this isn't the case for the majority of owners, so selecting the best method of getting keys to renters is an important issue.

Lockboxes come in all shapes and sizes and in varying degrees of complexity, so if you choose to use a lockbox, make sure it is a simple one. Phone calls on a Saturday evening from tired renters who are struggling with a lockbox after a long journey can be stressful for all involved.

Arguably, the best option is a keyless entry system that replaces the existing lock on an exterior door. Typically, these allow two codes to be set — one known only to the owner and caretaker/property manager, and one that is changed for each incoming rental party. Setting the code to the last four digits of the renters' home phone number means they are less likely to forget it, and having the number changed each rental week gives the owner peace of mind.

The only drawback of using this type of system is that it is battery powered. You will need to remember to change the batteries regularly and to have a key available for your guests to use as an alternative.

Other types of lockboxes offer push-button access to keys or are the more complicated sort requiring a dial to be turned back and forth to complete a letter code. When choosing your lockbox, consider the time of day your renters might arrive and ensure it is easy to use and placed in a location that offers good light for nighttime arrivals.

If you have chosen to hand over the keys in person, have a fallback plan in case your guests are delayed.

"Our guests were due to arrive at 4 p.m., and we were all ready for them. And still ready and waiting at 7 p.m.! We'd arranged to meet them, do the guided tour, and hand over the keys, and we didn't want to leave the place unlocked with the keys inside. So, we decided to stick around and wait. They eventually arrived just before midnight. Apparently they had left their house on time but stopped to pick up a few supplies on the outskirts of the city in an area they were not familiar with. The whole family went in the store, and when they came out the car had been towed for illegal parking. Although they had money and a cell phone on them, all details relating to our house had been left in the van. Needless to say we were all tired and frustrated.

"We now have an emergency plan and have a lockbox where we can leave the key if our renters are late to arrive. We still like to be there but it is not so important that we have to sacrifice more of our free time to hang about."

Most property management companies offer monitoring services consisting of regular checks of your property and reports on potential security weaknesses. They also act as key holder for monitoring purposes.

"We had an alarm system fitted in our property and opted for a monitoring service with our caretaker nominated as key holder. Last winter, we had a call from the security/alarm company to say they had been trying to contact the caretaker but had got no response. The temperature had become low enough to set off the cold alarm. Fortunately, we were able to get another neighbor to go in and raise the temperature; otherwise we might have had real problems with burst pipes. We've since decided to use a 24-hour service company as we know there will always be someone there if we have a problem."

Another advantage to having the property checked regularly is that you'd have someone to deal with storm damage. Some maintenance companies will automatically check your property after a storm as part of the package. This offers great peace of mind as the weather can be pretty unpredictable at times, and often extreme. It would be an unsettling experience to drive up to your vacation home for a weekend to find the last storm had blown down a tree across your roof. There goes your relaxing weekend!

12
GENERATING RETURN VISITS

"If you don't do it excellently, don't do it at all. Because, if it's not excellent, it won't be profitable or fun, and if you're not in business for fun or profit, what the hell are you doing there?"

— *Entrepreneur Robert Townsend*

One of your major goals should be to establish a regular clientele — guests that come back again and again, book a year in advance, come for out-of-season weekends, and rave about your property to their friends, relatives, and work colleagues. They see your place as their own piece of paradise for the time they are there, look after it wonderfully, and act as a free marketing and advertising service for you.

> "We have several families that book with us year after year. We know them so well now, some of them even carry out minor repairs and maintenance voluntarily, mow the lawn, and generally look after the place as if it was their own. They have a genuine pride in it looking its best. When they come in the winter, the power bill is usually lower than when we have other guests staying — we put it down to them having a feeling of ownership, even if it is just for a weekend. They turn down the heating when they go out, and follow all our guidelines for fuel economy."

Generating return visits from guests requires some effort on your part. It isn't just a matter of guests liking your vacation home, and you hoping they'll come back. Sometimes it works that way, but, as one of your primary goals should be to generate out-of-season income, you need to find additional methods of encouraging them to return. Since it's human nature for people to enjoy feeling wanted, and to have the impression they are "extra-special guests," there are a number of ways to do this.

EXCEED EXPECTATIONS

> "My wife's hushed 'Oh my God' said it all when we walked in the door."

This quotation about a first impression really does say it all! And this is what every owner should be striving to achieve. In most cases, rental guests have expectations that are built from very little information. Often it is based on a few photos on a website and a brief text listing. However brief the detail, they will generate a set of expectations that must be met or the first and most important impression will be one of disappointment and anger. Meeting and then exceeding those expectations are the foundation for creating raving fans. What follows are four key starting points.

Accurate description of all aspects of the property

This can't be emphasized enough. The last thing you want to happen is to be accused of misrepresentation, so make sure all your web listings and paper marketing have a bare-bones accurate description.

Up-to-date photos

You will want to use photos that show your place at its best, of course, but if there are any aspects of the property you would prefer not to show, the message is clear — do something about them before you rent. If you can't be transparent in your marketing materials you will risk being accused of hiding the less positive aspects.

Clean, clean, clean, then clean again!

High on the list of must-haves for rental guests is a clean property. And by clean, they mean spotless. And that goes for the outside and well as the inside. Swept decks, cobwebs removed from siding, and clean windows are a must. Attention should be paid to every part of the interior from ceiling fans to window frames, bathroom tiles to the inside of kitchen cupboards. If you give your guests nothing to complain about you will reap the benefits.

WOW your guests from the moment they arrive

People are most likely to remember the first few seconds and the last few seconds of an experience. These give the most memorable impressions, and you can create the first impression with outstanding cleanliness, a few decorative touches, and an appeal to all the senses. Good smells; soft music playing; visual triggers such as flowers in summer and an open fire in winter (but only if you are there to greet them, of course!) — these will all contribute to feelings of comfort and well-being.

STAY IN CONTACT — WITH THEIR PERMISSION

Many people will appreciate being informed of special offers, seasonal events in your area, improvements you make to your property, and any other information you feel would stimulate their interest to book again. However, please make sure you ask your renters if they would like to hear from you — and don't bombard them with emails. Three or four times a year is enough to remind them of the great time they had on their vacation

Birthdays and anniversaries

If you know your guests celebrated a birthday or anniversary while they were at your vacation home, send them a card well in advance of their next celebration offering a special weekend. Including tickets to a local concert or negotiating a discount for them at a nearby restaurant could be enough to convince them to return (and to tell lots of other people about how great you are!).

If you had honeymooners staying, remind them in advance of their anniversary that you have the property available for them and offer a discounted rate.

Activity breaks

Take note of what is written in your guest book and promote themed breaks to those clients who have mentioned particular activities. Skiing, fishing, cycling, and hiking are a few activities that offer opportunities to market out-of-season weekends.

ASK FOR THEIR FEEDBACK — THEN THANK THEM FOR IT

Ninety percent of people who have a complaint about a product or service never let the provider of the product or service know. However, on average, each of them will tell as many as ten others about their disappointment. The statistics on customer satisfaction are very clear about this. If you can capture the negative response and deal with it positively, you will have a more loyal client than one who was satisfied at the outset. If you've ever been in a situation where you have complained and it was handled positively, then you'll understand the slightly odd customer-service adage "a complaint is a gift." It gives you the opportunity to show that you can bounce back from negative feedback and transform a complaint into a positive outcome.

Of course it's up to you, but it's saddening to hear vacation home owners just dismissing a complaint with, "Well, we never had anyone complain about that before," particularly when they are not interested in finding out why their guests were unhappy in the first place. It would just be so much easier to spend a little time discovering why their perception was so different from yours. This is exactly what customer service is all about.

To gather useful feedback, you'll need a well-constructed questionnaire that will let your renters tell you what they loved about your property and their vacation, and also provide you with detail on those areas they felt could do with improvement. Before you do this, though, think about the last time you were asked to complete a questionnaire. First, did you bother at all? Time is precious, and if you don't see any benefit, you might not waste the few minutes it takes to complete the form. Most likely, there was some incentive to return the form, even if it was simply a self-addressed and stamped envelope. It takes a high degree of motivation to fill in a form, and then pay for it to be sent back.

Research has shown the highest response rates for surveys are when there are incentives to return them, such as a gift or discount on future purchase, so you might want to consider ways of doing this. Just providing the postage may be enough.

WHAT TO PUT IN A QUESTIONNAIRE

Your questionnaire should be designed to get the maximum amount of information from your guests about what they liked and didn't like about your vacation home, and indeed the surrounding area. This information will give you an indication of how people perceive your property and what you could do to make improvements. You might want to ask the following questions:

- How useful was the guest guide?

- Were the directions accurate and easy to follow?

- What was your overall impression of the property? If it didn't meet your expectations, can you explain how so? How could we correct this impression?

- What did you enjoy most about your vacation?

- What would you change if it were your place?

- What could we do or provide to make it even better?

- Did you visit any local places, attractions, restaurants, stores, etc. that you would recommend others visit, or avoid?

You can probably think of many more questions to ask — these are just suggestions. There is a sample questionnaire on the CD.

If you have included a children's quiz in your cottage pack (the author's Nature Watch quiz is included on the CD), have the quiz returned to you with the questionnaire. If you have offered a prize for the best response this will work even better, as it will be the guests' children who make sure it is sent back to you!

Another item you can ask your guests to send back is a copy of their best photograph of their vacation to put in the "Fun in the cottage" folder, or on the wall.

Ask for testimonials

Have a space on your questionnaire where guests can make an overall comment about their vacation or a specific aspect of it. Put a tick box next to the space, and ask them to mark the box if they are happy to have their comments put on your website or in your next brochure or leaflet. Many people *are* quite happy for you to do this, but you must ask first. If you do decide to use the testimonial, contact them again to reconfirm their agreement, and send them a transcript of the text you are planning to use. Thank them once again for their comments.

KEEPING IN TOUCH

Think about offering an out-of-season discount for each referral a guest makes that results in a booking. Giving a 10 percent (to up to 50 percent) discount works very well. Remember, this is filling up the space where normally the property would be unoccupied.

And don't forget to send your leaflet on fall, winter, and spring breaks, offering a discount on these out-of-season short breaks. You can do this via email as well.

13
HANDLING COMPLAINTS

However well you manage the upkeep of your vacation home, supply additional items to add value, and believe you have thought of everything, there will still be complaints. Most books and articles on customer service tell you that soliciting complaints allows you the opportunity to fix things and make amends which in turn will keep your customers coming back, as they feel you have listened to them and taken their feelings seriously. To a great extent this is true, and is the main reason for asking your guests to complete a questionnaire after their stay. Not only does the feedback tell you that you are doing things right, it may also serve to point you in the direction of changes you could or should make for the better. If you then thank the client for their feedback and let them know you have made changes as a result of it, they will be far more inclined to come back.

It is strange that some people feel compelled to make some negative comment even when it is clear they have had a wonderful time. This often amounts to something minor; however, think carefully before deciding to ignore it. For example, the following comments are just a few of the odd complaints received from owners' questionnaires:

- *The kettle didn't boil fast enough*
- *There was only one bathroom* (there were only two people staying)
- *The bathroom was too small for six people*
- *The TV was too small*
- *The lake was too cold for swimming* (early May)
- *We couldn't sleep properly because it was too dark* (or too quiet)

Many comments like these can be taken with a pinch of salt and chuckled over. However, it is worth noting all of these and updating your guest guide accordingly. Yes, you may even have to go as far as mentioning that it does get dark at night and there are no streetlights, and that the ice on the lake melts in mid-April, so it may not be warm enough to swim in until at least mid-June! Don't leave anything to chance. If you have just one small bathroom, make sure you say so; if there is poor reception on the TV, make it clear (no pun intended) and suggest your guests bring videos or DVDs with them; and state clearly and concisely any procedures your guests need to follow to operate cottage systems.

Avoid making any assumptions about your guests' knowledge about being out in the country, particularly if they are from overseas or from a different state. They may not understand some of the terms you may use.

One couple telephoned the owner of their rented property to ask where the well was, and how they should draw water from it! The guest guide had indicated that the well water was good for drinking, and they thought this was a different source from the water that came out of the faucet in the kitchen.

SERIOUS COMPLAINTS

What constitutes a serious complaint?

"We had guests staying for the May 24th holiday. They phoned us on the Saturday to say the bugs were so bad they couldn't go outside, and they wanted their money back! It was difficult knowing what to do, but in the end we offered them a free weekend in the fall — with no bugs. We did sympathize but had assumed they would know it was blackfly season. We now make it very clear when people book for May or early June that the bugs may be out and we accept no responsibility for them! We're not sure we did the right thing by giving away another weekend, but they seemed very happy and did book another weekend in February."

Most complaints of this nature can be forestalled by anticipating things that could go wrong and making contingency plans to deal with them, or identifying and briefing your guests on things that are just a fact of cottage life.

"We love our lake — it's small and motors aren't allowed so it's also very peaceful and safe for children. We make sure that all our potential guests know this. The last thing we want is people booking for two weeks then arriving with a trailer and jet skis, or a boat. They could always launch at a nearby lake, but it could still be very disappointing for them if they expected our lake to be an active motor lake."

In general, if you are honest about any shortcomings your property may have, you won't surprise your guests with anything to complain about. And if they do, listen to them, keep calm and rational, and see if you can compromise in any way.

14
THE GUEST GUIDE

A guest guide is an essential tool for both you and your guests, and it is definitely worth spending some time to get it just right. If your guest guide is comprehensive and covers every eventuality, your guests will have all the information they need for a trouble-free stay, and you'll feel confident that you have covered every angle. This is not to say that you must write a massive tome, the very size of which would put anyone off even before it is read. Rather, it should be a concise directory with a good index and laid out in a well-organized and structured way.

Your guide should include the following:

- Clear instructions for operating fireplaces, wood stoves, and any appliances

- Recommended operating temperatures for hot tubs and pools, and general "rules" of use

- Your policies on smoking, telephone usage, pets, additional visitors, and cleanup

- Garbage collection and recycling details, including directions to the local landfill if required

- Useful information on local sights and activities, including a calendar of events

- Contact details for you or your property manager or caretaker

Using a folder with plastic sleeves will keep the manual clean and tidy, and if you update your local event list every couple of months you can keep it current without having to redo it totally. Get a folder with a see-through pocket on the front, and insert a sheet with a good picture of the property and a clear title, for example, "Clearwater Lake Cottage — Guest Guide." (There is a downloadable template on the CD so you can create your own personalized guide.)

Send a summarized version of the guest guide to your guests a month before the rental period, together with directions and key location information.

Do keep your cottage folder up to date.

"We rented a place in early summer and found the information pack included a list of events from three years ago, and information on appliances that were no longer on the property. There was very little tourist information — apart from several leaflets on the local ski hill and snowmobile rental, which were not too useful as it was June! When we suggested to the owner that he might update it, he said he usually did for his summer guests but hadn't got round to it yet. This made us feel very welcome!"

CONTENTS OF THE GUIDE

So what goes into the manual? The following is a recommended list of things to include.

Index

As well as a comprehensive index, use section dividers, each with a front page listing what is in each section. This means guests can find what they need to know very quickly.

Welcome and introduction

A friendly opening is a must — avoid starting with a list of things your guests must or must not do. This can come later using a softer introduction. Include any interesting history on the area, for example:

How Gooderham Got Its Name

The village of Gooderham was called Pine Lake prior to the early 1870s, when a representative of the Gooderham & Worts distillery visited and reputedly left a case of whiskey at each of the three hotels in the bustling community. The Pine Lake residents were so impressed with this generous gesture, they voted to change the name from Pine Lake to Gooderham.

Add a proviso at the end of the introduction that goes something like this: "Although everything in the property is in good working order as far as we know, please contact us, or our nominated representative, within the first 24 hours if you discover a problem with anything or any damage you believe we should be made aware of." You do not want to discover damage after they have left and have them respond that it was like that when they arrived.

Phone numbers

As well as the cottage telephone number, list the numbers for yourself or your caretaker, the local police, fire, and ambulance, the local hospital, and any other emergency service.

Also useful is the telephone number for guests to check current local fire restrictions.

The local area

This is a brief summary of what is available locally. (More details can be included in the "Places to go and things to do and see" section later on, where you can include leaflets and brochures.) Include:

- Brief description of local area and communities

- Location of and distance to the nearest general store, supermarkets, gas station, post office, and tourist office

- Location of and distance to the nearest town that has malls and movie theaters

- Recommended restaurants

Don't forget to include any irregular or seasonal opening or operating times here as well.

Arriving

In this section include the information your guests will find useful upon their arrival. This is particularly important if they are required to park in a certain place or enter through a particular door. Make sure these details are included in the summary information pack you send to guests before the rental period commences. Include:

- Location of the keys

- Immediate need-to-know information such as where light switches are — useful for arriving in the dark!

- Where to park vehicles

- What's in the fridge

Systems

You may have particular instructions about the water and sewage systems of your property. Here you may want to be firm about what you allow. Remember that what may seem second nature to you may strike your guests as being overcautious. People who are used to urban drainage and water systems may not have encountered the joys of a septic system or the need to conserve water. The general recommendation here is to spell out the worst that will happen if the instructions aren't followed. You can soften the message in a variety of ways, perhaps by using humorous cartoons or clip art (freely available on the web or included in many word processing software packages).

The text below gets the message across without laboring the point or making it too negative:

Water and Septic Systems

In common with most "cottage-type" properties, The River House is fed by its own well, and water is pumped into the house via an electric pump. You may hear the pump running after the toilet is flushed or while faucets are running. You'll notice a black pipe running into the river which is the overflow from the well. The water quality has recently been assessed as excellent although it does have a brownish tinge to it, which is caused by the high iron and mineral content. If you would rather drink bottled water, there is a water cooler with two containers of water supplied.

And another example:

The cottage is served by a septic system. These systems are designed to cope with human waste and two-ply (or less) toilet tissue only; if you attempt to dispose of any other forms of waste, including sanitary products, disposable diapers, cotton buds, cotton wool, or even tissues, a blockage WILL occur. When this has happened in the past, it has caused considerable expense for us and inconvenience for guests as a plumber may not be immediately available to resolve the problem. If there is a problem of any sort with the septic system, please contact the caretaker immediately.

Appliances and operating instructions

You don't need to include operating manuals for all your appliances — keep these separate, and just tell your guests where they can find them. However, it is useful to list all the equipment they may want to use, to note any quirky aspects of operating this equipment, and if necessary create specific instructions, particularly if there are any energy-saving techniques. For example, Europeans, and in particular British guests, are used to stoves with a separate broiler. It may seem strange to include instructions on how to use the broiler on your stove — you might add a section or text box specifically entitled "Additional notes for our overseas guests." Considering that 99 percent of British households have an electric kettle, and many of these are cordless, it's no wonder that cottage owners regularly receive calls asking where the kettle is kept.

If you have a laundry room, include instructions for general washing, and a reminder to empty the lint collector in the dryer regularly.

Microwave ovens have become more and more complex and they are not necessarily as intuitive as they should be. To avoid the late-night phone call asking how to get it working, include a brief guide on the most common functions. The same goes for the TV.

Outside the cottage

Here you can bring up the barbecue — mention where the nearest propane supplier is and include a reminder to clean the grill after use to deter unwelcome animals looking for leftovers. Make it clear what outside "toys" can be used by your guests. If you have watercraft, list what they are, together with a note on the legal requirements for their use. Letting your guests know they will be liable to a hefty fine if they take out the canoe without a life jacket and compulsory additional safety equipment will prevent any misunderstandings. Don't expect your guests to know about the rules of the water — they often won't, particularly if this is their first visit to a lakeside property.

English guests renting a cottage near Algonquin Park took the canoe out on the lake on their first day, were stopped by the water police, and fined heavily for not having the appropriate equipment in the craft. They had not been warned about this. Quite a hard lesson to learn on the first day of a vacation, and one that could have been easily averted if the cottage owner had been a little more thoughtful in his cottage instructions. Incidentally, the instructions he had provided were several years out of date, grubby, and found at the back of a cupboard after an extensive search.

As added value, you will have provided a selection of serviceable life jackets or PFDs (personal flotation devices) with your cottage name or your surname clearly labeled on them. Simply advise where these are kept and ask that they are returned there after each use. As PFDs should fit well for optimum safety, let your guests know that although you may have provided these for their use, they are responsible for making sure each member of the family has an appropriately sized one.

If you have instructions for the care of canoes, pedal boats, and so on, make that clear. For example, if you want watercraft removed from the water at the end of the rental, include this in your checkout checklist.

If your guests are likely to bring their own watercraft, offer information on boat launch facilities, local marinas, etc. Don't include any disclaimers here; this should be done on a separate form that your guests are required to sign.

Fire pits

You'll have included a telephone number for guests to check current local fire restrictions in your useful number list, so remind guests that they should call this number before they light a fire. If you allow fires, indicate clearly where the fire pit is and stress that this is the only place where a fire may be lit. If you don't do this, people might indulge their pyromania all over your property. It's also useful to identify where wood for the fire can be found. That will avoid the following situation.

"We had a group for the Thanksgiving weekend. We'd mentioned there was wood under the deck for use in the airtight fireplace in the lounge — the good stuff we had piled up for winter use. After they had gone, we arrived to find that half the wood had been used, and there was a huge burnt area down by the lake. They must have been up all night sitting in front of the blaze."

Keeping the critters at bay

Seasoned country cabin owners will know that what they really have is potential six-star accommodation for the local rodent population. However, with good precautions in place, rodents will find entry difficult if not impossible. Nevertheless, even with the strictest entry controls, there will always be those persistent little fellows determined to take up residence in your top-star rodent resort. We have found that it matters little what you tell your guests about their responsibility to act as bouncers to unwelcome guests — they will still leave doors open, and screens ajar. Just imagine the chatter of the outdoor mice community on changeover day: "Hey guys, this bunch are moving out — look, they've propped the door open. Line up behind me, and we've got a free run in the next time that guy heads out to the van with another bag." And then ... "Here come the next ones! They must be from the city too — and they'll have brought fresh food they'll leave on the kitchen counters overnight. Let's go for it!"

It may be that the first time you know you have a problem is when you get a call from your renters that they are overrun with the little critters. Get your caretaker to make an urgent visit to set traps, and remind your guests not to leave any external doors open. Since instructions about making sure doors are kept shut are very important, this is one of the few occasions when it is acceptable to put a notice on the door as well, to reinforce the point.

If you are leaving traps for your guests to use, include information on the best bait, and remind them to wash their hands thoroughly after disposing of the deceased. In addition, you may encounter the more squeamish guest who would prefer to use a "humane," nonlethal trap and then release their catch back into the wild. You might mention in your guide that said rodent will probably instantly return to its nest in the cottage and carry on as before, and that it is actually illegal in many places to release vermin into the wild.

Chipmunks can also be a problem, as most guests will see them as adorable creatures that will take a cookie from their hand. You know that once in the house they are very difficult to catch and evict, so educate your renters about prevention, as the cure can be time-consuming, not to mention fatal for the unwanted intruders.

Sitting outside my brother's cottage one afternoon, we were watching a furtive-looking raccoon checking out the neighborhood before climbing onto the deck of the cottage opposite and disappearing into the cottage through the cat flap. Two minutes later, the raccoon reappeared, on the end of the owner's boot. Landing several feet down the yard, Mr. Raccoon picked himself up, gave himself a shake, bounded up the stairs, and back through the cat flap where he met the boot once again. This time, the trajectory was a little higher, and it seemed to put him off as he shook himself down again and, with an attempt at dignity, wandered nonchalantly back into the woodland.

On a serious note, it is important to advise your guests against encouraging wildlife, however appealing it may look. This is vital with guests from countries where raccoons are not native — the UK, for example. Visitors will see them as cute little things and may even encourage them into the property — with dire consequences. Include instructions in your guest guide about keeping garbage either inside, securely placed in a lockable bin, or in a shed or outhouse. It's perhaps better to frighten them with the possible consequences rather than let them think they can make domestic pets of wild animals while at your home in the country.

Bugs and other flying creatures

Be honest about the bugs! Deerflies, blackflies, mosquitoes, ladybugs — ah, the joy of country living, and for longtime owners, they are "just one of those things." And, after all, the nuisance is far outweighed by the pleasures of life on the lake. However, you may well find you have guests who have not come across some of these irritating pests before, and therefore they need to be forewarned. This is particularly true with blackflies. Even if you can't forecast the season with much accuracy, it is better to be up-front about the possibility of blackfly swarms from early May through to mid-June.

Garbage disposal

This is another area where city dwellers need clear direction on what to do. If there is municipal waste collection, this is straight-forward; if not, instruction on garbage disposal is essential. How is it collected or where do guests take it to? Where do they buy pre-paid tags or find the landfill card? And outline your policy on recy-cling, particularly in areas where garbage disposal is restricted. As an example:

> **We are committed wholeheartedly to recycling and respect-fully ask you to be so as well during your stay in our cot-tage. The township issues fines for nonrecyclable garbage in excess of two bags per week. If you leave any bags in excess of this limit, the fines will be deducted from your damage deposit.**

Places to eat and things to do and see

With a little research you may be able to negotiate discounts for your guests at local places of interest and restaurants, particularly in the low season. Make a list of places to eat, and include a short description of the ambience and type of food to expect. If you have a visitors' book and encourage guests to write reviews of restaurants, mention this here. Don't forget that any negative rec-ommendations are also important in ensuring your guests don't have an unpleasant or disappointing experience.

Briefly describe the facilities and attractions of the local area and/or the local town. Including brochures and leaflets here is a good idea, but make sure to keep them seasonal and up to date. Maps, including those for local hiking trails, can be very useful.

Departure

Reiterate the stipulated latest departure time from the cottage and exactly how you want the place to be left. If you offer a cleaning service, ask guests to remove bedding from the beds they have used and place it in the laundry room, or wherever you want it left. You then know which beds have been used, which does make a changeover easier. Say where you want the key to be left and any locking-up instructions. Finally, draw attention to the cleaning checklist and say where you want guests to leave this checklist.

15
WRAPPING UP

By the time you reach this point, you should have a good idea about how you want to proceed with your vacation home rental business. Hopefully, you have made a decision on whether you are going to manage your rental by yourself, put it in the hands of a good rental agency, or perhaps use a combination of both. You have now decided on your marketing strategy, have a clear plan on how you will promote the weeks you have available, and are focused on how you will develop a good website. Now is the time to sit back and review all your plans and make sure you have everything documented.

Check off the following steps as you complete each one:

☐ Hold a brainstorming session

☐ Prepare a marketing strategy including a budget and plans for promoting the holiday rental

- ❏ Do an analysis of other rentals in your area for evaluating rental rates
- ❏ Do a property audit
- ❏ Research rental agencies
- ❏ Find contact names and numbers of web designers
- ❏ Select well-staged photos and text for the web listing
- ❏ Organize a booking system including availability calendar and rental agreements
- ❏ Prepare a cottage guide for renters
- ❏ Develop a list of contact numbers for tradespeople such as plumbers, electricians, general handymen, etc.
- ❏ Arrange for rental insurance
- ❏ Do a cash flow forecast
- ❏ Create a post-rental survey
- ❏ Develop a list of theme ideas for promoting the cottage out of season
- ❏ Make a list of ideas to add value to the rental package

If you have checked every item on this list, you're ready to go. It's important to make sure you're fully prepared, as the moment your listing appears on websites, people will start to call and all your systems need to be in place to handle the inquiries.

Above all, have fun doing this. You will meet some great people, help families enjoy their dream vacation, and create income along the way. Providing you have done the groundwork and are comfortable that you have done your best to prepare for any eventuality, you'll do just fine. So good luck, enjoy, and start that ball rolling!

The following checklists, forms, letters, and templates are included on the CD-ROM for use on a Windows-based PC.

Planning Tools

- Cost of Furnishings Worksheet
- Creating a Vision Worksheet
- Marketing and Sales Goals
- Rental Agency Comparison Chart
- SWOT Analysis
- To Rent or Not to Rent

Booking Management Tools

- Booking Confirmation Invoice
- Booking Confirmation Letter
- Deposit Return Letter
- Final Payment Letter
- Final Statement
- 5 Inquiry Response Letters
- Post-Vacation Questionnaire
- Record of Customer Inquiries
- Rental Agreement

Rental Property Toolkit

- Cleaning and Changeover Checklist
- Emergency Preparedness Worksheet
- Essential Items List
- Power Outage Information
- Template for Cottage Guide

Samples and Templates from Cottage Knowledge

- Annual Cash Flow Spreadsheet
- Client Tracking Form
- Nature Watch Quiz
- Rental Calculator
- Sample Marketing Leaflet

— and much more